MW00775249

"Doug Giles is a good man, and his bambinas are fearless. His girls Hannah and Regis Giles are indefatigable. I admire the Giles clan from afar."

– Dennis Miller

"Doug Giles must be some kind of a great guy if CNN wants to impugn him."

– Rush Limbaugh

"Doug Giles is a substantive and funny force for traditional values."

– Ann Coulter, best-selling author

"Doug Giles speaks the truth ... he's a societal watchdog ... a funny bastard."

– Ted Nugent, rock icon

Pussification

The Effeminization

of the American Male

Written by

Doug Giles

Copyright 2016, Doug Giles, All Rights Reserved

No part of this book may be reproduced, stored in a retrieval system, or transmitted by any means without the written permission of the author.

Published by White Feather Press. (www.whitefeatherpress.com)

ISBN 978-1-61808-145-2

Printed in the United States of America

Cover design by David Bugnon and mobopolis.com

Editing by Steve Pauwels and Constance M. Hill

Bio photo by David Cartee

Scripture taken from the HOLY BIBLE, NEW INTERNATIONAL VERSION®. NIV®. Copyright © 1973, 1978, 1984 by International Bible Society. Used by permission of Zondervan. All rights reserved worldwide.

Scriptures marked KJV are taken from the KING JAMES VERSION (KJV): KING JAMES VERSION, public domain.

Table of Contents

Dedication

This book is dedicated to my grandson, Hamish.

May your motto forever be, *contra mundum*.

"Secretly, everybody's getting tired of political correct-
ness, kissing up. That's the kiss-ass generation we're in
right now. We're really in a pussy generation."

– Clint Eastwood

Introduction

As you can tell, this book is not a long philosophical treatise on how American males morphed into prancing candy-asses.

I don't have the time, nor the desire, to write some massive book trying to pinpoint the who, what, when, where and why of how males became sad, sackless wonders.

I'm too busy working hard and playing hard to do that for the *Tickle Me Elmo* reader who demands a mega-detailed book or he'll throw an intense hissy fit.

Look, if you're in need of a more exhaustive tome regarding the emasculation process of the postmodern male, then allow me to refer you to the book titled, *I'm A Pussy Who Likes Reading Long Books Versus Actually Kicking Butt in Real Life* by Imma Jackwagon

Now... granted... this book might be brief, but it's filled with road-tested historical wisdom and maxims guaranteed to put sand in your mangina and offend you deeply, but will, in the final analysis, if believed and obeyed, produce a life that doesn't suck like an airplane toilet.

To be clear, my dear reader, my motivation for penning this book is simple: I want to find your inner-child and kick his little ass.

I'm going to shake and bake you, little brother.

I'm going to take your rose-colored glasses off, grind them into powder right in front of your weepy face and fish slap you into the rarified air of the testosterone-leader fog via the pages of this book.

Doesn't that sound fun?

Oh, on a serious note... this book could be life's last wake up call for you.

For some, this could be the voice of God saying ... "Hey, dipstick, wake the heck up!" Or something to that effect.

By the way, when God speaks to me, and it's often, it's usually in an angry, high-pitched, Chinese accent. It's true. It's freaky but hey... at least he's communicating.

So... how's that for an intro?

Pretty tasty, eh?

I've purposely set the bar high for you boys and this book is not for everyone.

Matter of fact, the more I think about it, you probably shouldn't read this book because, more than likely, your helicopter mommy raised you to forever be a mamma's boy and this book will just make you mad and cost you more expensive therapy sessions at the *I've Chosen to Forever Be a Blathering Over-Coddled Pussy Clinic.*

So... put it down and walk slowly away.

Do it now.

Yes, proceed no further because what lies ahead is going to be rougher than grandma's breath. Especially, if you cudgel off any and all responsibility for your haggard existence.

Matter of fact, if you're into blaming others then you should definitely put this book down and walk away because this read will be more torturous to you than a Celine Dion concert is to me.

You know... the more I think about it... the more I seriously question whether or not you have the mettle to handle the rock-strewn, root-choked, demon-infested road that leads out of the swamp of Pussville and up to the sacred mountain of Mantown.

Therefore... you should probably quit reading at this moment and climb your 26-year-old pathetic self back up on mommy's lap and resume chewing on her leathered nipple and have her wet nurse your sad, little existence right up to and through your mid-life crisis.

(PLEASE NOTE: Here's where Doug pauses during his live presentations at men's conferences and watches the whiners walk out of the meeting while he smokes a cigar and waits patiently for God to thin the herd so he can get down to the serious business of making whiners warriors.)

Hey, look at you.

You're still reading (or listening).

Congrats!

Maybe there's hope for you.

Indeed, there may be hope for you if...

1. You are deeply ashamed that you have flown so often to Puss-ville, when difficult times came, that you now have a lifetime platinum status on Bitch-Air.

2. You are more frustrated than a white, 13-year-old Baptist boy at a Nicki Minaj concert.

3. And yet, in spite of your frustration and anger, you still believe that God and life has more to offer you; and you're big enough not to blame others but to acknowledge that your life pretty much sucks right now because you've regularly chosen the path of the pusillanimous.

So, buckle Crispin. Get ready to morph from a man-child to a real man.

Also, keep this book handy and read it at least every six months because the pussy spirit, like a demon, always tries to come back and possess its old home. Finally, buy at least five copies for your buddies because you don't want to be hanging out with pussies, as I'll discuss later.

By the way, this book was primarily written as an audio book so don't flip out if you think it looks more like a script than a book, because it is a compilation of rants meant to be read by *moi*.

Doug Giles
Somewhere In Texas

Section One

Well Hello, Pussy

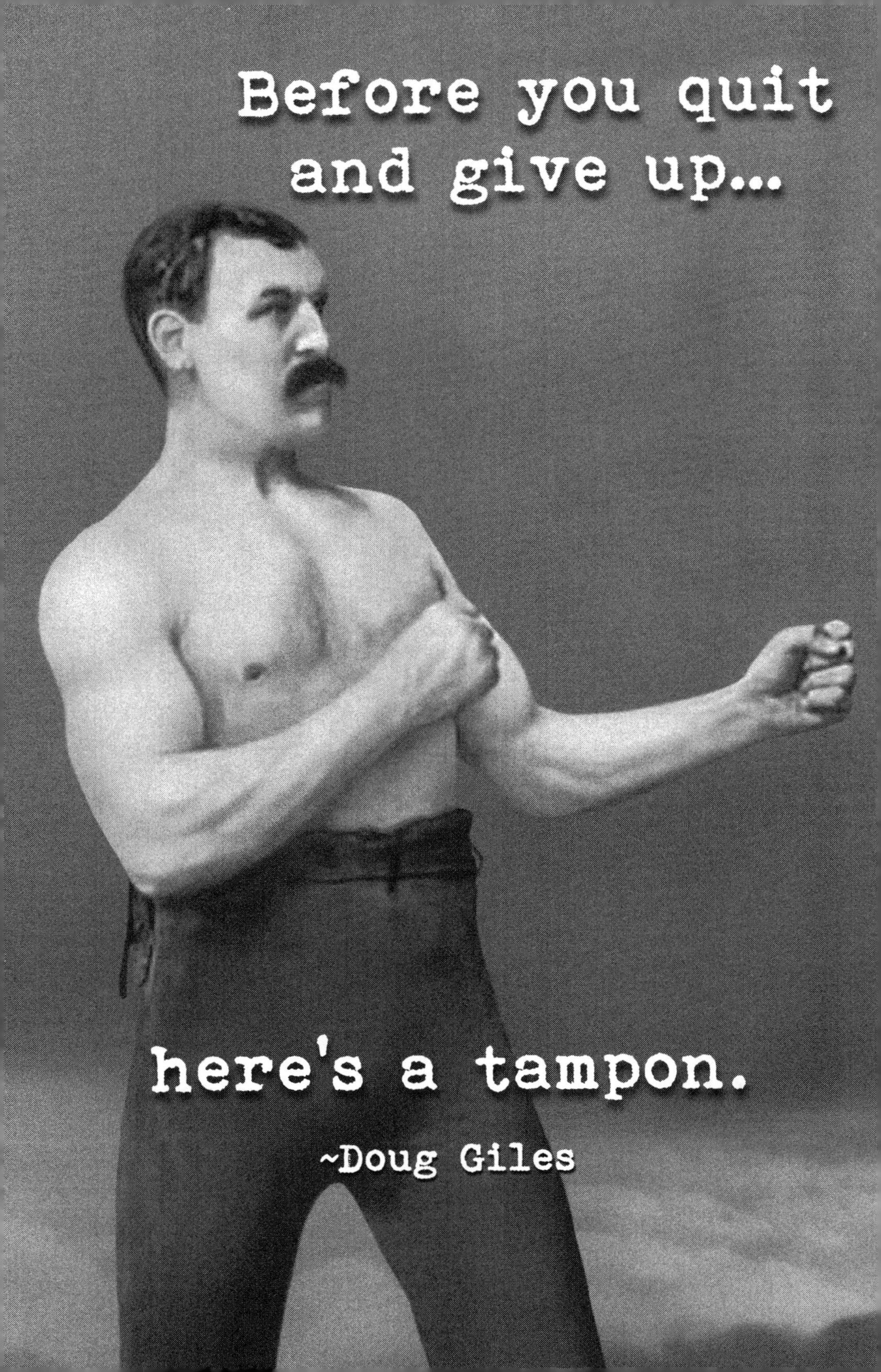
Before you quit
and give up...
here's a tampon.
~Doug Giles

Chapter 1

Meet Crispin

Meet Crispin

This book is written for "Crispin".

"Who the heck's 'Crispin,' " you ask?

Well, Crispin is the catch-all name I've given to males who can be defined ...

1. As twenty-somethings who've been over-coddled by mommy.

2. Who're also devoid of real dudes in their life and are ensconced by radical liberal chicks, overbearing aunts and/or lame quasi-male males.

3. They also take notes and life cues while watching *Keeping Up with the Kardashians*.

4. In addition, they find solace at the Mall instead of the woods or a museum or on the gun range or gutting a deer.

5. And lastly, they're the kind of XY chromosome who goes to a "User-friendly Church" and are being "life-coached" by a hipster youth pastor named Sebastian whose hair puts the

"gel" into evangelical.

6. Oh, I almost forgot. These half-baked sweeties also think Hillary would make an "epic president".

Sad… right?

However, it's not entirely gloomy for all of the cowed and craven Crispins because the fat lady hasn't sung… yet… on some of their gelded glide paths.

Indeed, the salvageable ones that I'm out to save with this book are those who're starting to wake the heck up, finally, and realize they've been listening to the wrong people for most of their lives.

Yep, something deep inside them is making them feel very stupid that they're now twenty-five years old, wearing skinny jeans, a girl's deep V-neck T-shirt, a man bun and they sport more bangles than an Ubangi warrior.

> Crispin is realizing
>
> …
>
> He's screwed.

Not only that, but Crispin is also waking up to the fact that no chick worth her salt wants to date him. The only female he can attract is some dippy, unwashed, communist, chunky-tuna chick who's majoring in White Male Micro-Aggression Theory and The Problem of Whiteness, with a minor in Queer Musicology.

From an occupational stand point, it's beginning to dawn on Crispin that it's now becoming hard for him to find a job outside of Starbucks because real bosses …

• Don't like his multi-pierced ears.

- Won't allow him to take off work because his cat is sick.
- Call BS when he claims he's having "parasympathetic menstrual cramps brought on by being super close to his female roommate, Sha Nay Nay."

Spiritually speaking, this thing he calls his "journey" has also taken a turn for the worse. He's now questioning "if God is dead" because all that crap Joel Osteen told him would come true if he said it often enough hasn't, and his life is filled with these "icky things" called "difficulties".

> Crispin can't get a date or a decent job!

Yep, life is starting to bite Crispin on his manscaped ass.

And Crispin no likey it, but now… Crispin's at a fork in the road. A *very* important fork in the road.

And nowadays… amongst the boys… the road he must take is definitely the road less traveled.

Here's the two options which lay before this semi-awakened wanker at this juncture.

> Crispin stands at a crossroads in his life.

The road to the right leads up to the high mountain of Mantown, which is a glorious place of greatness and accomplishment, where eagles soar, and fops and dandies fear to tread.

The road to the left descends down to a slough of despond called Pussville, where dreams and dreamers go to die. A place where losers group-hug

3

each other while they play the victim and blame other people as they endure a grueling government-assisted, abysmal life of mediocrity with a big side of envy.

Betwixt the twain stands yours truly with this book that has all the subtly and TLC of a sledgehammer.

Doug Giles, the butt-kicking, sledge hammer of Truth is your friend.

Some of you young dolts need the sledgehammer and should think of me, therefore, as your personal Gunnery Sergeant Hartman, the Grim Reaper, your worst enemy and your best buddy all rolled into one cigar-smoking obnoxious ass-kicker.

Finally, if you're a pussy and you intend to stay in the warm, wet extended womb of Pussville, then you and I will not get along and you will hate this book. Which is cool with me. It's no sweat off my back. It's your sad life that's going to reek. So go for it. Throw your hissy fit and ignore me. I dare you.

However, if you're one of the Crispins I just described, who's waking up, allow me to encourage you to continue plowing a mad path out of Pussville and into the rarified air of Mantown.

Be warned, however, that leaving your life-sucking friends and your sucky-life decisions is going to be a tough little monkey.

Yep, the climb to Mantown from Pussville is all up hill, sometimes very treacherous; and there are very few resting points. But who cares, eh? It's the tough stuff that makes one great, right? Of course I'm right.

I shouldn't say "pussy" but "wussy", instead?
That's exactly what a pussy would say.
~Doug Giles

Chapter 2

Pussification Defined

Pussification Defined

PUSS-I-FI-CA-TION: The act, or process, of a man being shamed, taught, lead, pastored, drugged or otherwise coerced or cajoled into throwing out his brain, handing over his balls and formally abandoning the rarified air of the testosterone-leader-fog that God and nature hardwired him to dwell in, and instead become a weak, effeminate, mangina sporting, shriveled up little pussy.

* From *The Doug Giles 2016 Dictionary of Grow the Hell Up, You Pussy*!

Some of my fairer brethren have instructed me to use the terms "wussy" and "wussification" when talking about one being a pussy who has gone through our culture's emasculation process of systematic effeminization.

To that I say… "Oh, Please." That is exactly what a pussy would do.

Indeed, and FYI for my genteel readers who need to nut up, shut up and move up and out of Pussville; both pussy and its derivative, pussification, are slang for a ten dollar, word namely, pusillanimous. It's an adjective meaning one who's timid; a dandy

who shows a lack of courage or determination. In other words...
a pussy.

Pusillanimous is a word that you've probably never heard of
before because your vocabulary is lacking breadth and depth because you're an intellectually lazy dolt. For the inquiring minds,
the Greek word for pusillanimous is the word "deilos" which is
pronounced "day loss". Which makes total
sense because there are many "days lost"
to people, nations and families who've
been pussified, right?

Pussification is
not a dirty word

...

get over it.

Of course I'm right. So... rest as-
sured, fair reader, that when I say one is
a "pussy" I'm not referring to a woman's
sweet lady parts.

Indeed, ladies and genitals, I would
never insult a woman's vagina by com-
paring it to a person with no guts, who whines all day, sits around
and cries like a chick for years over nada; who will blow anything
out of proportion and create insane drama in order to forget about
their sad and miserable lives.

No, my friends... a women's vagina is a valuable, pleasur-
able, useful, and muscular life-giving organ – unlike a whiny and
sheepish man child.

Now, when I call one a pussy please note that just because...

1. You don't look like The Rock.

2. You don't shoot machine guns.

3. You don't have as much body hair as Michelle Obama.

4. You don't run with the bulls of Pamplona.

5. You can't bench press your body weight...

...that doesn't necessarily mean that you're a pussy; because
pussies come in all shapes and sizes.

Matter of fact, I know big "bad-ass guys" who're physically

terrifying but are inwardly terrified when it comes to facing the spiritual, physical, political and cultural monsters they're confronted with in their own Valley of the Shadow of Death.

Yep, I'm buddies with geeks, artists, nerds, intellectuals, preachers, hacktivists, policy wonks, little schoolteachers, missionaries, housewives, cancer victims, peeps with debilitating setbacks and others who, outwardly, don't sport much bravado, but inwardly they are full on butt-kickers in this game of life.

Ergo, get it out of your head that I'm lauding some kind of knuckle-draggin', Cro-Magnon like mook in this book. That's not what it's about at all. Oh, heck no.

So relax.

Just because you don't look like Dwayne Johnson doesn't mean you're screwed.

The thing I'm most concerned about is not so much an outward machismo but inward chutzpah, where you defy setbacks and forever cease to listen to this pathetic, debilitating and insipid boo-frickin'-hoo spirit defined herein.

> **Real men don't have to be physically strong.**

Yep, my goal with this timely and vital tome is modest: I'm out to save the planet. One pussy at a time.

Listen, if some of you males don't grow the heck up and stop listening to the wilting voice in your whirring-tin-brain, then your life and our nation is going to be more screwed than Lindsay Lohan at Lamar Odom's Roofie, Vodka, Cocaine, Crack & Acid Party. Here's my promise to you... the pussy:

If you read and obey what I tell you to do in this book you'll die a happy man and your friends and family won't have to lie about your horrendous pussy life at your miserable pussy funeral.

This book is about your being a man.

It's about doing something worthy of your DNA.

Hopefully, God willing, if you're obedient, then you'll leave a wicked scar on mediocrity's haggard backside. Yep, in order to salvage this third rock from the sun from all the mayhem misandrists and evil weeds have foisted on our globe, we need men who would be men.

You can bet your mamma's last buck that's stored in your pink piggy bank next to your Ryan Seacrest poster in mommy's basement that justice won't be served, truth won't prevail, benevolence won't be apportioned properly and the planet will not be bettered... if... YOU... stay... a... pussy.

> I'm out to save the planet – one pussy at a time.

Synonyms for pussy include, but are not limited to: wimp, sissy, dipstick, pansy, loser, coward, dillweed, bitch, weak, lame, baby, chicken, whiner, punk and weakling.

Section Two

Four Signs You've BEEN Pussified

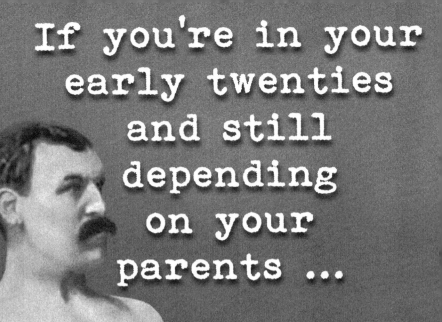

If you're in your
early twenties
and still
depending
on your
parents ...

then you're a pussy.

~Doug Giles

Chapter 3

You're Not
A Provider

Sign # 1

You're not a provider

Here's some disturbing bunkum via The BBC.

Call this "more proof" that I'm right and that Generation Pussy is morphing into a man-bun-sporting, pusillanimous pajama boy faster than a corn dog dipped in Vaseline goes through Rebel Wilson's tailpipe.

Check this out:

A 22-year-old college dandy, George Fellowes, claims he gets his period every month.

Yes, you read that right.

A "he" named "George", who sports an actual penis, unashamedly spewed that sputum to the BBC.

Yep, According to the BBC, Fellowes says he's been riding the crimson wave "without bleeding" for the last couple of years.

Someone throat punch me and tell me this is a bad dream.

So, how did Georgie Boy get this malady?

Well, I'm glad you asked.

Jorgé says his affliction arose because, "he's so close to his best friend and flatmate Amber-May Ellis that he gets cramps when she comes on each month."

You can't make this crap up, eh?

Numbnuts continues, "I think it's a psychological thing because we're so close, we feel the same emotions," he said. "If you're hanging out with someone and you're really close, I think it's only natural your hormones would sync up like clockwork every month," cried Georgie.

Fellowes further stated, "I get pain in my lower abdomen and in the groin area. I get super moody, really erratic and angry with most of my friends... I'm not really one for a cry but during that time of the month I'm an emotional wreck."

F-F-Fellowes is even bold enough to confess that he's taken sick days off work because of his imaginary "period."

Dear God. I feel defiled just reading that scat.

Excuse while I watch a Clint Eastwood flick, smoke a Safari Cigar and drink a dirty martini to cleanse my soul.

Okay... I'm back.

Is this a man we're talking about? Really?

Now, as gross as the aforementioned is, herewith are four scarier and more substantive signs that a dude is endangered by the evils of emasculation.

My advice, little Crispin, is to put on a cup... because it's about to get rough.

Herewith is the first of four sure-fire signs you've been pussified.

1. You're Not a Provider. If you're in your early twenties and you're not paying for most, if not all, of your stuff, then you're a pussy.

Awww... did that hurt your feelings? It did? You know why it hurt? It's because you're a pussy!

Oh... I know. You have "special reason" why you're crippled.

Let me guess: it's because daddy didn't make it to your 3rd grade play starring you as Peter Pan because he was trying to pay the bills and keep a roof over your precious head.

Consequently, according to your youth pastor, his absence is the causal reason you've been permanently dis-enabled of all normal maturity traits which are common to the male species; and therefore, that is why that thing you call a "life" now blows more than a turbo-charged, nitrous-oxide-enhanced, Husqvarna 50 Pro Gas Backpack Leaf Blower.

Look, boys: all able bodied dudes should be bringing home the bacon.

They should be making the flow.

They should be bringing home some Benjamins.

Y'know... takin' care of business.

In case you're not understanding what I'm getting at, the next time you and your male buddies have a play date that entails dressing up like Beyoncé and doing some karaoke, select her song *Independent Women.*

While you're gettin' all sassy... struttin' around and snappin' Z's, pay close attention to the lyrics and try to live out what Queen Bey espouses in that tripe of a song, you pussy.

Author's note: For this next sentence, pull out your journal, Dear Crispin, and write the following into your diary.

Being a man, in the classic sense of the word, entails not being a government-handout sponge or some mommy/daddy dependent dipstick. You dig?

> **Your father is not responsible for your pussyhood. It's you.**

So, what am I gently alluding to heretofore?

It's this: get a life, Crispin.

Start making some righteous cash.

Quit waiting for things to "happen." Go out and make it happen.

Get off your mommy's breast. Like... in... now.

Check this out: Being dependent is the epitome of being pathetic.

It's disgusting and you're ridiculous if that's how you live.

Matter of fact, if the founding of America were somehow up to you, our nation would be called the United States of Pussies, because what you're smoking ain't the kind of moxie our marvelous union was founded upon.

> A real man takes care of himself and his family.

Finally, ladies... if you're dating some douche who can't or won't draw his wallet on a date, then say "Hello" to Mr. Pussy.

And no... before you start trying to defend him... he's not a "special case". He's a mooch and he probably will never change. If you doubt me, girls, then just ask your married girlfriends who're married to a worthless toad.

You have been forewarned. Proceed at your own peril.

Oh, and one more thing: if you're married and you're not providing for your household... guess what you are? If you guessed a pussy, you guessed right. Especially if you're a Christian. The non-pussified Apostle Paul put it this way:

> "If any provide not for his own, and specially for those of his own house, he hath denied the faith, and is worse than an infidel"

(1Timothy 5:8 KJV)

I bet you indolent, male, Christian don't have that verse on a refrigerator magnet stuck to your fridge, do you?

Yeah, I didn't think so.

Here's the only exceptions as far as I'm concerned: If you've had your body riddled with shrapnel during a war, or got burned beyond mobility, or some other true disability whether by war, or accident, or by

> Ladies, don't be fooled by a man who won't pay his own way.

serious birth defect, or via a brutal hand of fate, then of course, we the people, should take care of you. Especially if you've sacrificed greatly in the line of duty.

However, if that ain't you... then you need to get busy providing for yourself and your loved ones. Like in right now.

A real man will figure out how to make cash and will do whatever the heck it takes to provide.

So, pony up, sister. Play the man. And yes, it is your job to take care of your family. It's called responsibility.

> Crispin, it's time to grow a pair and hit a home run for your family!

In addition, if you're married and have a family, not only should you provide money for your casa but you should also provide time to be with them, being a source of love, wisdom, humor, trust, forgiveness, balance, discipline and vision.

Awww... what's that I hear?

Is that the whimper of a weenie whining about that being a tall order to fulfill for a frail fop like you?

Well, garsh, little sweetie, what did you imagine adulthood to be like? Some extended version of the masturbatory teens you spent ensconced in a velvet jumpsuit living at mommy's house?

Sorry, Crispin. It's time to grow a pair and forever leave the little leagues and become a provider of physical goodies.

If you can't
defend yourself
or others ...
I predict you'll soon
lose your girlfriend
to a guy who can.
~Doug Giles

Chapter 4

You're Not
A Protector

Sign # 2

You're Not a Protector.

Back in the caveman days, if some cave bastard from some other tribe tried to steal a man's brontosaurus ribs, or the wheel he just invented, or his hot cavewoman, or they tried to harm his snaggle-toothed cave brood, the man under attack would find the nearest pterodactyl bone and commence beating the living crap out of said thievenous cave thug.

And he would usually beat the moron to death. Like in splat.

And if he didn't kill the cave thug, he would've definitely left one of those massive, cartoon-sized lumps on their head.

The aforementioned was what was considered normal for man up until the 1960s when the man-haters began the systematic emasculation of the male collective, trying to eradicate any and all semblance of this primal, protective funk from their constituent junk and turn them into a squealy, 21st-century-hipster liberal.

Indeed, primitive man understood that to him belonged the responsibility not only to provide for himself and his family, but also the duty of beating the shiitake mushrooms out of any man or animal that threatened his *familia*'s existence.

The men who had this protective prowess; who did not curl up in the corner of their cave in the fetal position behind a stalagmite, suck their thumbs and wet their hamster loincloths were the ones who were afforded the right to propagate.

> The primitive human race had the man thing down to a deadly art form.

Yep, the primal man did not need to rely on The Cave Police Department, or The Cave National Guard, or Brinks Cave Security Systems.

Oh, heck no. Check it out...

He was the front line of defense.

He was there to jack you up.

He was the first responder.

He was the security system.

He was the standing army.

He was the cop on duty.

It was his job to protect everyone, everywhere and at all times, and God help the dumb ass if they transgressed or trespassed on that which was under his care.

Now, fast forward several million years to now and the ubiquitous metrosexual males who'd run screaming like... well... a metrosexual male when serious shiite hits the fan in their presence.

No doubt, one of the many sad things about our nation's multitudinous, iPostured, twenty-something males is that a great swath of them don't know how to protect themselves, much less their girlfriends or wives or their poor kids, should things go to hell in a handbasket.

A true dude will beat the be-Jesus out of someone who threatens his family.

A true man will double-tap the center mass of any jackass that seeks to hurt or harm loved ones and innocent people.

Now... if you feel like you're lacking in this protective spirit I have four simple things to make you come alive as a full-fledged bad-ass. So... pull out your journal, Crispin, and start taking notes.

> A true man will protect his family.

To wake up this latent protective instinct that God hard-wired you with you must do the following:

1. Go get punched in the face.

Like in tonight. Don't put this off. Have someone knock the crap out of you. You won't die and you'll learn you're more resilient than your mommy, daddy, teacher, pastor, priest and/or therapist thinks you are. If you can't find someone to punch you in the mouth; at least have your feisty sister slap the snot out of you. Oh, and by the way, most real men and women don't trust someone who's never been punched in the face. It's true. It's science. Ask around.

> Look cool and have a plan to kill everyone in the room.

2. Learn how to fight, STAT.

Now that you've been punched in the face you should immediately enroll in martial arts or boxing or both and train for at least ten years. Make certain you find the best of the best in your town or city to train you and do not quit until you become a force of nature.

3. Learn how to use weapons.

I'm talkin' guns, knives, baseball bats, nunchucks, whatever. Learn how to expertly wield them. Once you've mastered these protective tools, buy an arsenal of them and have them close by at all times because... you... just... never... know.

4. Keep your head on a swivel.

Be alert at all times. Constantly be aware of your surroundings and have General James Mattis's motto tattooed on your psyche, namely, "Look cool and have a plan to kill every bad guy in the room." And remember, when seconds count the police are minutes away.

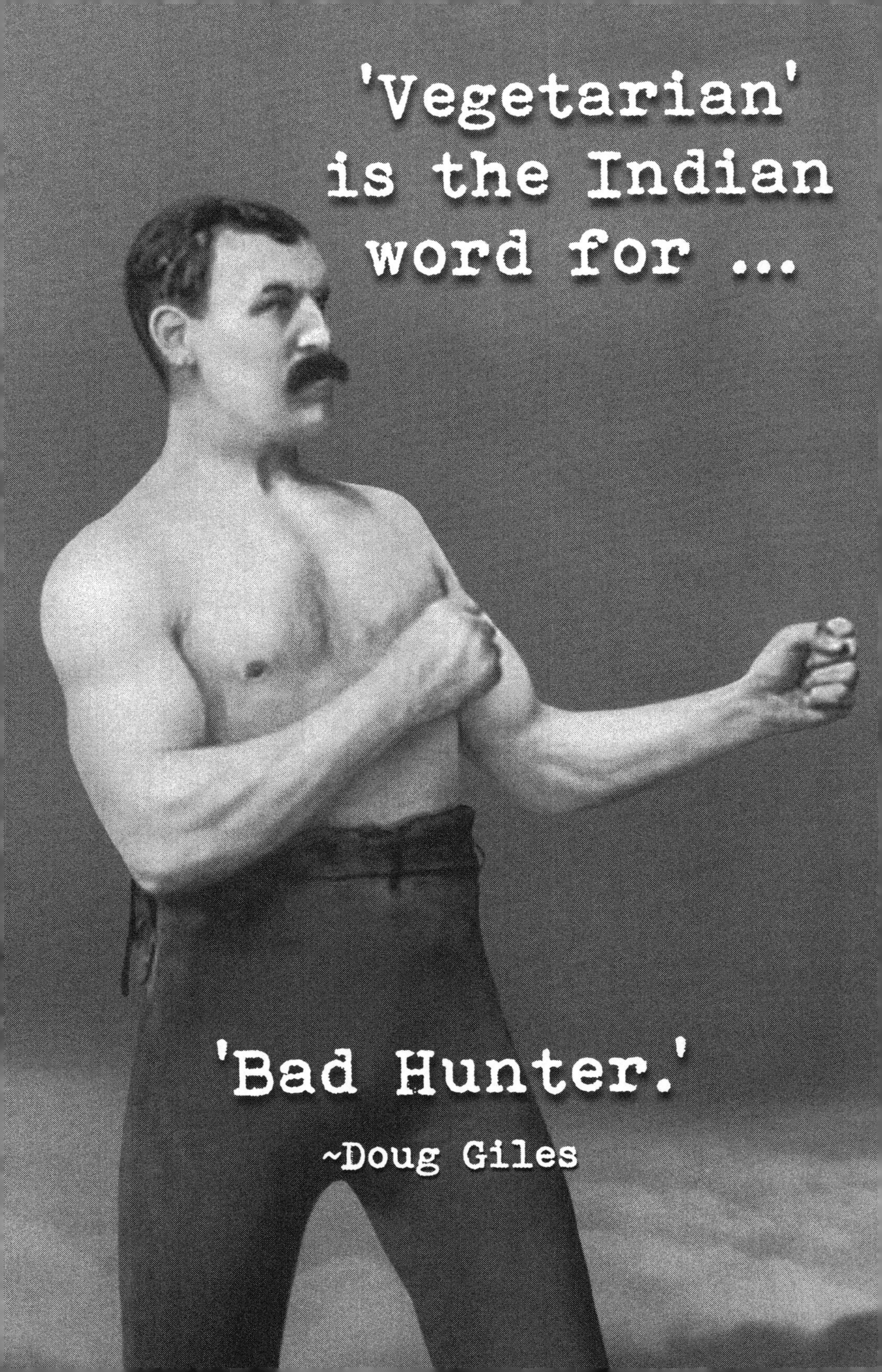
'Vegetarian' is the Indian word for ...
'Bad Hunter.'
~Doug Giles

Chapter 5

You're Not
A Hunter

Sign # 3

You're Not a Hunter.

One tell-tale sign that a male's balls have been snipped, or slowly eroded, and he's formally in line to get outfitted with a big, whopping, weepy mangina is that he does not hunt.

I think it's truly pathetic, sad and unfortunate that a stack of men doesn't know how to hunt or fish any longer when it is indelibly dyed into their DNA as carnivores.

Dude: What the hell are you going to do when the zombie apocalypse goes down?

How will you and yours survive because you're not eating any of my vacuum-packed venison. That's for sure. And good luck finding your precious tofu and edamame beans to sustain you and your liberal lover when you're fleeing from flesh-eating zombies, you non-hunting Nancy.

Look, man: you're a predator whether you like it or not.

You are a flesh-eater.

That's why you have eyes on the front of your skull and canines.

Why do think God or evolution or whatever you want to believe in physically outfitted you with fangs and eyes forward?

Do you think it's chiefly because God wanted you to be able to see a Starbucks at a great distance, order a Venti Skinny Macchiato with pumpkin spice and then slurp and chew on that long, green straw like a pussy?

No.

Of course not.

Indeed, the eyes were placed forward on that useless skull of yours and the canines were placed in your whiny mouth in order for you to see prey, kill prey and eat prey.

I'd like to take a wee bit of a rabbit trail for the next nine-hundred words with a special message just for the ladies:

I'll never forget the summer of 2005, when my gorgeous wife walked into my office, while I was cleaning my guns and talking to my two hunting bros about our next adventure, and asked me to hunt a buffalo.

"Honey, can you shoot me a bison?" she said. "We'd get a freezer full of meat and a bison shoulder mount would look beautiful on our walls," she said.

Let's see... a wife asking her husband, in our paranormal state of aggravated pussification, to go hunting, bank some grub and then have the beast mounted and displayed proudly upon the walls? All I had to say to that unforgettable scenario was... Yahtzee!; and, of course, Thank you, Jesus!

> **In the Great Zombie Apocalypse ... vegans die first.**

After she asked me to go hunt an American bison she smiled and left.

Be still, my beating heart.

My friends sat there gobsmacked... stupefied... that a wife would actually ask her husband to hunt. I know some folks in Texas and Alaska don't find that odd, but in Miami, and from what I've experienced with hunting and couples from around the globe, that was some *Twilight Zone* stuff.

My single buddy who witnessed this divine event asked if she had an unmarried sister. My married *compadre* chimed in and said, "Hell would freeze over before my wife would ever ask me to go hunting."

I can't lie to you, folks. I felt a combination of blessedness and sorrow: blessedness because, hallelujah, I didn't marry some testicle-snippin', carpy-wife-from-hell; and sadness because of my single mate's grim situation of slim-pickedness and my married *amigo*'s state of hen-peckedness.

Because I hunt and fish a lot, and I write about my pursuits afield, I've been blessed to know many professional hunters, guides and outfitters from Alaska to Africa; and I've been instrumental in hooking people up on epic adventures from boar hunts to cape buffalo hunts and everything in between. I've

> A good woman helps a good man become even better.

also been on the receiving end of hearing guys who'd like to hunt tell me they can't go hunting because... wait for it... "Their wife won't let them."

"Their wife won't let them"? What kind of grown man actually says something like that?

Look, I get wives saying, "Honey, I wish you wouldn't go hunting brown bear in Prince William Sound this spring because you haven't paid our mortgage in the last four months."

What I don't get is a petulant wife hunt-blocking her husband who has paid the bills and has taken care of business; and said chick still throws a fit about his wanting to hunt or fish. To me... that's bullcrap.

Allow me to let you highly feminized, controlling lasses who've watched way too much *Desperate Housewives* in on something about husbands that we don't dig; and why you might be single again soon, very soon. Are you ready? Check it out. Here are 11 things husbands hate ...

Husbands hate...

1. When you throw them under the bus in public.

2. When you remind them of their past failures.

3. When you unload on them as soon as they walk in the door.

4. When you expect them to be just like your girlfriend.

5. When you expect them to read your mind.

6. When you treat them like your child.

7. When you unload the big guns on them at 11 p.m.

8. When you compare them to that "perfect guy" at church.

9. When you give them the silent treatment.

10. When you use sex as a weapon.

11. And when you complain about their going hunting and/or fishing.

By the way, a happily married woman wrote 1-10. Number 11 is all mine.

Not only do men, who would be men, hate the aforementioned, but also God, according to the Scriptures, is sympathetic to the plight of the husband who is married to a contentious dame.

> Your wife won't "let" you hunt? That's a joke ... right? Please tell me it's a joke.

Check it out...

Proverbs 21:9 (KJV) Better to dwell in a corner of a housetop, than in a house shared with a contentious woman.

Proverbs 21:19 (KJV) Better to dwell in the wilderness, than with a contentious and angry woman.

Proverbs 25:24 (KJV) It is better to dwell in a corner of a housetop, than in a house shared with a contentious woman.

Proverbs 27:15 (KJV) A continual dripping on a very rainy

day and a contentious woman are alike.

Ouch, baby. Very ouch.

Ladies, real men are naturally hard-wired to be hunters. True men are providers, protectors, hunters and heroes. To stymie this is to effectively neuter your dude and keep him from what God made him to be; and diminish him to the realm of the effeminate. Trust me, girls; if and when the crap hits the fan, you don't want some brow beaten tinkerpot who can't put meat in the pot should the economy and country go to hell.

> 11 things husbands hate ... this is the short list.

Finally, if I was a woman – and I'm not, even though I do like Kate Hudson movies – I'd thank the good Lord my husband was a hunter. At least he's not gambling, or going to strip clubs, or banging Rhonda the overly tattooed Hooters waitress. At least he's getting away from the concrete, the mall, the plastic and Facebook and interfacing with God and nature and getting his soul restored. At least he's part of hands-on conservation through hunting; and if he's a good dad he's bringing his kids along in this grand pastime of global stewardship; and he's putting high protein/low-fat food on the table versus that chemical-laced, store-bought poison the indoor boys eat.

> God doesn't like nagging wives any more than He likes pussies.

So, relax, ladies. Bless the hunter/angler husband that you have. Feel a sense of pride that you have an alpha male who can both bring home big dollars and big deer. Surprise him this week and ask him to go hunting and fishing. Sure, initially he'll think you're cheating on him and want him out of the house or that you fell and hit your head; but when he sees you lighten up you'll find the tension die down and that could help your tedious union. And at least you can take pride that you're not married to a metrosexual.

Oh, and one last ditty for the single dudes… if you hunt or want to hunt and you're dating some girl that doesn't like hunting, pick your junk up and run like a banshee chewing leather in the opposite direction. If you don't, then don't whine when the anti-hunting chickens come home to roost.

You're welcome; and you may make the counseling check out to "Doug Giles."

A pussy looks for an excuse to run from battles ...

but a warrior looks for the opportunity to throttle the enemy.

~Doug Giles

Chapter 6

You're Not
A Hero

Sign # 4

You're Not a Hero

I've been reading Steven Pressfield's musings on warriors and warfare and this quote struck me like Kourtney Kardashian punching Scott Disick when he wore the wrong scarf to the You're a Big Pussy Soiree.

> "The Spartans do not ask how many are the enemy but where are they."
>
> *– Plutarch, Sayings of The Spartans*

And that, my friend, is one of the big differences between a warrior and a wimp.

A pussy, you see, looks for an excuse to run (I/we don't have "enough") but a warrior looks for the opportunity to throttle the enemy.

The strange thing is that nowadays, in our aggravated state of pussification, one would call the inquirer of how many foes are arrayed against them "a wise calculator of the risks involved" and whether or not they are able to contend with what they have at hand or if they should retreat. When, in reality, such questions, oftentimes, are nothing but cowardice masked in some shrewd sounding horse hockey that doesn't make one sound like a neutered newt.

That mindset afflicted an old friend of mine from Cali who was way smarter than I when it came to books and business but would always talk himself out of startups and personal goals because he always viewed how "insurmountable the obstacles were" rather than how he could possibly tackle his mountains.

> "They're on our right; they're on our left; they're in front of us; they're behind us. They can't get away *now!*"
>
> —*Colonel Chesty Puller*
> *United Sates Marine Corps*

This attitude equated this brilliant, book-smart buddy's being a stay-at-home dad versus an alpha-male Viking.

How sad.

Here's the bottom line, folks: if anything is worth doing it will be fraught with sick hurdles. That's life, Crispin. The sooner you take on the warrior mindset, the quicker you'll be talking about great victories. So, from now on, talk yourself into the battle instead of how you can get out of the battle.

Oh, one last thing. Allow me to crow a wee little bit.

One day my buddy and I pulled up to a store for a beer run. We were just minding our own business when we saw this dude, who was being chased by several employees, come hauling ass out of the store we were about to go into.

I had no idea what was going down but as two squad cars came squealing into the parking lot I did some quick math and deduced that a robbery just occurred.

I saw the culprit duck down a side street that the employees and cops didn't see, so I bolted out of the car, whistled for the cops and began chasing the bandit with the police in tow.

The thief, thinking he'd escaped notice, slowed down to a fast walk, not knowing that Miami's finest and I were sneaking up on him.

To make a long story short we blinded sided the perp, tackling him on the sidewalk, and expedited his sorry backside to jail.

Why did I do it?

I don't know.

I guess it was instinct.

> A hero, by instinct, springs into action when help is needed.

Sometimes you just put two and two together and have to kick some unrighteous ass.

My wife called me a hero. Enough said.

When's the last time your wife called you a "hero"?

Zzzzzzzzzzzz.

Just in case you've forgotten.

(From dictionary.com)

hero – [heer-oh]

noun, plural heroes;

1. a person noted for courageous acts or nobility of character:

Example: He became a local hero when he saved the drowning child.

2. a person who, in the opinion of others, has special achievements, abilities, or personal qualities and is regarded as a role model or ideal:

Section Three

Bullies Love Pussies

Islam is
to Peace ...

What Rosie O'Donnell
is to sexy.

~Doug Giles

Chapter 7

Islam Loves Pussies

Islam Loves Pussies

> **Dear Pussy,**
>
> **This Sinister Death Cult LOVES Your Being a Politically Correct Pussy**

Here's something that pissed me off.

Did you know that the largest university press on the planet warned its writers last year not to speak of "pigs or pork" because it might offend... wait for it... the Muslims?

Yep, the Oxford University Press (OUP) said that their books must now bow to the Religion of Peace and avoid mentioning bacon or "anything else which could be perceived as pork," the International Business Times reported.

And get this: This effeminate edict was revealed during a round-table on "free speech" during BBC Radio 4's Today show.

Check this out – and I quote: "I've got a letter here that was sent out by OUP to an author doing something for young people," BBC's presenter Jim Naughtie stated.

Jimmy continues, "Among the things prohibited in the text that was commissioned by OUP was the following: Pigs plus sausages, or anything else which could be perceived as pork."

Which mean, I guess, that Oxford Press will now have to scrap that Rosie O'Donnell bio they were working on.

> Question: Can you believe that politically correct poppycock, ladies and gents?

All I have to say about that pathetic mitigation of the freedom of the press is, "Hello, Pussies."

> **Score one for Islam and none for British pussies!**

Oh, I almost forgot, that little soiree on "free speech" came on the coattails of Muslims slaughtering Parisian cartoonists in the now infamous Charlie Hebdo terrorist attack.

Yep, instead of telling those murderous bastards to go screw themselves, and if they don't like our cartoons or pepperoni pizza then they can move back to whatever Suckistan they hail from; OUP, which is an apropos acronym if I've ever heard one, bans the mention of bacon.

Indeed, The Oxford University Press, like many others, especially in Europe, has tripped over themselves to not offend the constantly offended Religion of Peace.

Score one for Islam and none for British pussies.

By the way, the Oxford University Press also included "The Jews" in that easily offended, anti-bacon, bunch. But you and I both know that it's not the Jews who act like fascistic jackasses towards a Gentile's lunchmeat selection. It's Islam, and only and always Islam, which flips out over the presence of Jimmy Dean breakfast links.

And that, my friends, is how creeping Sharia slowly cooks the Western Civilization frog by slowly enforcing their unreasonable rules on freedom-loving people.

Islam loves it when the lame roll over for their ridiculous requests and that's why I wrote the following...

DEAR PUSSY: This Sinister Death Cult LOVES Your Being a Politically Correct Pussy

"You have enemies? Good. That means you've stood up for something, sometime in your life."

– Winston Churchill

I don't know who started the politically correct pussification process of the male collective, but I'd like to find them and pistol whip them into next week with my S&W Model 29 for ruining our planet.

Why am I irate this glorious morning in the Texas Hill Country?

Well ... simply put: it's because males are being shamed, taught, lead, pastored, drugged, schooled, coerced and cajoled into throwing out their brains, handing over their balls and formally abandoning the rarefied air of the testosterone-leader-fog that God and nature hardwired them to dwell in; and instead they've become a weak, effeminate, mangina-sporting, shriveled-up quail. That's why.

> Political correctness is Islam's staunchest ally.

I hate this emasculated culture.

It's pathetic and pervasive and its effects on society are deadly. As in, literally. I'll explain later.

If you think I'm full of specious doo, then sit your skinny-jean-wearing butt down in your Hello-Kitty chair and watch a little TV; and pay close attention to the male characters, whether fictitious or "real", and tell me with a straight face that you'd want these preening dandies to have your back in a gunfight.

A couple of weeks ago I took the aforementioned TV Puss Test and here's what I observed being directly and indirectly shoveled down our male pie-holes regarding what "being a man" meant:

- Man buns and glitter beards are now "all the rage".

- The Boy Scouts of America have banned water pistols.

- Boys at this one school aren't allowed to play soldier any more.

- A university banned fencing because a sword fight might break out.

- Brotox is becoming popular among men.

- Some lame-ass company now has "Diet Whiskey" for "men".

- A thirteen-year-old boy was actually punished for being a hero.

- A study showed that men are now beginning to talk like girls. Like in... OMG.

> **Political correctness and freedom cannot coexist.**

- A gym removed its squat rack because it was intimidating to its squishy clients.

I saw on Facebook an old, pro-toy-gun TV advert that sure as shizzle wouldn't fly today.

And most male actors are not men in the classic sense of the word that I grew up with, but rather male tinkerpots that are required to cry on cue.

And that was just scratching the pop culture surface; and it doesn't include the uber-effeminate "Christian" TV zombies or our craven politicians on the Left and the Right.

That said, I believe one of the rankest places our pussification shows its browless noggin is in regards to Islam. These ridiculous and antiquated people want to conquer and kill us and we're told to not point that out.

Back in the day, our news sources, military leaders and politicians wouldn't mince words about Nazis, or Stalin's thugs, or Japan's shiitake; but God forbid that we should say that Islam spawns terrorism more than fried eggs and refried beans make Gwyneth Paltrow gassy.

When ordered to jump by Islam, the MSM asks "how high?" on the way up!

Yep, one of the most egregious forms of effeminization, and one that yields up the most ubiquitous examples, especially during Obama's reign of terror as Puss-In-Chief, is the politically correct fetal position the "media", and especially liberal politicians, take when discussing bat-crap crazy Islam. It's pathetic.

Here's how lame some men have become when facing Muslim Mayhem at home and abroad. I grabbed these headlines from my website ClashDaily.com. Check it out:

• Brits Cancel Mohammad Cartoon Exhibit Because It's Too Offensive

• UK Pool to Ban Bikinis and 'Islamically Inappropriate Swimwear'

• US Embassy Removes July 4 Celebration Out of 'Respect for Islam'

• NYT Whines About How Our Bad-Ass SEAL Team 6 Kills Terrorists

• NYT Says, Chris Kyle 'Insane'– Bruce Jenner 'Courageous'

• College Students Demand That 'American Sniper' Be Banned from Campus Because It's Too Offensive.

As Col. Ralph Peters famously said, "My God, ISIS is taking over the Middle East, and our President can't even say 'Islamist

Terror'."

Daily, I see the most "You-gotta-be-kidding-me" excuses made, and cover given for, Muslim rapes and violence in Europe. It's disgusting and it's turned deadly in Sweden, Belgium and Paris all via the intentional kissing of Islamic butt.

> **Stop kissing Islamic butt. Instead, we should be kicking it!**

Personally, I think Europe is done. Their culture has become too PC and the invasion of Islam now too expansive for them to recover.

Finally, Leftists and Islam need you to be cowardly, docile and house-trained. They must eradicate a man's masculinity in order for their evil machinations to thrive; and they're doing a good job of making males spineless weasels aplenty... a society of frightened men.

Here's my easy prediction:

"until men start acting like men and defy these religious Islamic monsters, then you and I can expect more massacres, rapes and invasions, and loss of our sacred liberties; and all because of our culture's systematic pussification."

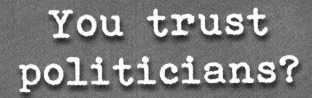

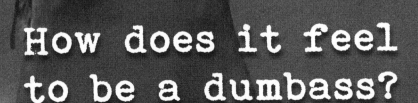

Chapter 8

Big Government Loves Pussies

Big Government Loves Pussies

In case you didn't know this, Crispin, our nation was founded by brilliant, freedom-loving heavy weights.

It's hard to imagine that nowadays because our country is currently being deconstructed by moronic, liberty-choking, light weights also known as "politicians". In particular ... Liberal politicians.

Liberals, you see, don't mind what you do as long as they approve.

They're kind of like King George III and his inbred dipsticks in that regard. Or, for a more current example, they're somewhat like Islam with their fascism, sans the billy-goat beards and the suicide vests.

That said, our current crop of freedom-stranglers isn't entirely made up of Leftists as there are many who claim to represent the Right who also believe it's their duty in life to make our lives beholden to big- government, power-hungry dillweeds.

If our founders were around right now they would stomp on this current crop of micro-managers like a narc at a biker party. Literally.

Yep, from a freedom standpoint, our founders were a horse of a different stripe.

They hated control freaks.

They loathed tyrants.

They trusted government about as high as Rosie O'Donnell can pole vault after her 5pm feeding.

> **Rebellion to tyrants is obedience to God.**

Indeed, once our original framers got this incredible country up and officially cranking they began to cobble together a seal, a picture, a motto, and an emblem, which would encapsulate what they had concocted on fresh American soil.

Benjamin Franklin, being the rebel he was, wanted it to be a picture of Moses confronting Obama… I mean, Pharaoh, when Moses demanded Pharaoh cease his enslavement of Israel and let God's people go. This image was to be encircled with the phrase "Rebellion to Tyrants Is Obedience to God." Thomas Jefferson liked the motto "Rebellion to Tyrants is Obedience to God" so much, he used it on his personal seal.

Today, especially during BHO's be-damned days, the symbol the Left would concoct to represent their "American Dream" would be a pic of a dependent, 45-year-old, multi-pierced, Transgendered, whatchamacallit breast-feeding off a big, old, saggy, milk-dried, government dog tit: a veritable dependent, indebted and enslaved stooge of the machine from the cradle to the grave.

So, what's my point? Well, it's this: we're pussies.

All of us.

We have not the singular mettle that made this grand experiment in self-governance tick. I'm guilty and you're guilty and we can blame corrupt politicians, puff our chest, and scream at MSNBC all day long, but the truth is… we let politicians screw us. We traded our freedoms, prosperity and our original roots and moorings for mediocre comfort over duty; and we were daft enough to believe them time and time again.

Matter of fact, if Thomas Jefferson, not to be confused with George Jefferson, is in heaven right now, and he's able to peer through some celestial portal and behold the bullcrap Barack has saddled this nation with – a country, by the way, that Jefferson labored to make independent from tyrants – then I would bet that Thomas is more ticked than a boar that just had its balls clipped.

How do I know Jefferson would loathe our big government goobers and seek to jettison our Jester-In-Chief? Well, it's principally via Thomas' musings – musings that, for the time being, we're still afforded the wherewithal to access; principles that also happen to have made our nation great and that used to be taught in our school system.

Plow through the following from one of our nation's illustrious framers' quills and try to tell me with a straight face that Jefferson wouldn't have sought to derail our current, oppressive leaders via tooth, fang and claw:

1. The spirit of resistance to government is so valuable on certain occasions, that I wish it to be always kept alive. It will often be exercised when wrong, but better so than not to be exercised at all. I like a little rebellion now and then. It is like a storm in the atmosphere.

> Americans must regain the "mettle" to stand up to tyrants.

2. It is error alone which needs the support of government. Truth can stand by itself. Subject opinion to coercion: whom will you make your inquisitors?

3. A free people [claim] their rights as derived from the laws of nature, and not as the gift of their chief magistrate.

4. If people let the government decide what foods they eat and what medicines they take, their bodies will soon be in as sorry a state as are the souls of those who live under tyranny.

5. The multiplication of public offices, increase of expense be-

yond income, growth and entailment of a public debt, are indications soliciting the employment of the pruning knife.

6. And can the liberties of a nation be thought secure when we have removed their only firm basis, a conviction in the minds of the people that these liberties are the gift of God? That they are not to be violated but with his wrath? Indeed I tremble for my country when I reflect that God is just: that his justice cannot sleep forever.

7. No freeman shall be debarred the use of arms [within his own lands or tenements].

8. The principle of spending money to be paid by posterity, under the name of funding, is but swindling futurity on a large scale.

9. Laws that forbid the carrying of arms... disarm only those who are neither inclined nor determined to commit crimes... Such laws make things worse for the assaulted and better for the assailants; they serve rather to encourage than to prevent homicides, for an unarmed man may be attacked with greater confidence than an armed man.

10. In questions of power, then, let no more be heard of confidence in man, but bind him down from mischief by the chains of the Constitution.

11. I hold it that a little rebellion now and then is a good thing, and as necessary in the political world as storms in the physical.

12. It is of great importance to set a resolution, not to be shaken, never to tell an untruth. There is no vice so mean, so pitiful, so contemptible; and he who permits himself to tell a lie once, finds it much easier to do it a second and a third time, till at length it becomes habitual; he tells lies without attending to it, and truths without the world's believing him. This falsehood of the tongue leads to that of the heart, and in time depraves all its good disposition.

13. I am not among those who fear the people. They, and not the rich, are our dependence for continued freedom. And to preserve their independence, we must not let our rulers load us with perpetual debt. We must make our election between economy and liberty, or profusion and servitude.

14. The disease of liberty is catching; those armies will take it in the south, carry it thence to their own country, spread there the infection of revolution and representative government, and raise its people from the prone condition of brutes to the erect altitude of man.

15. Every government degenerates when trusted to the rulers of the people alone. The people themselves, therefore, are its only safe depositories.

16. Still one thing more, fellow-citizens — a wise and frugal Government, which shall restrain men from injuring one another, shall leave them otherwise free to regulate their own pursuits of industry and improvement, and shall not take from the mouth of labor the bread it has earned. This is the sum of good government, and this is necessary to close the circle of our felicities.

17. A private central bank issuing the public currency is a greater menace to the liberties of the people than a standing army. We must not let our rulers load us with perpetual debt.

18. Born in other countries, yet believing you could be happy in this, our laws acknowledge, as they should do, your right to join us in society, conforming, as I doubt not you will do, to our established rules. That these rules shall be as equal as prudential considerations will admit, will certainly be the aim of our legislatures, general and particular.

19. I have been happy... in believing that... whatever follies we may be led into as to foreign nations, we shall never give up our Union, the last anchor of our hope, and that alone which is to prevent this heavenly country from becoming an arena of gladiators.

20. I know no safe depository of the ultimate powers of the society but the people themselves; and if we think them not enlightened enough to exercise their control with a wholesome discretion, the remedy is not to take it from them, but to inform their discretion by education. This is the true corrective of abuses of constitutional power.

Finally, I believe until "We The People" resurrect the aforementioned motto and mantra by which the likes of Franklin and Jefferson clipped along, namely, pardon my redundancy, "Rebellion to Tyrants is Obedience to God", then we will continue to see this land morph into a cartoon of what it was intended to be.

Yep, until we internally get to where our founders were, in particular, believing like they did, that it was their divine duty to vehemently oppose oppressors and not kiss their enslaving backside, we will continue to eat crap and content ourselves with ever decreasing freedom and the land of the free and the home of the brave will irreversibly morph into the land of the bound and home of the slaves.

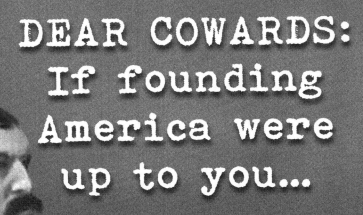

Chapter 9

The Constitution of the United States of Pussification

The Constitution of the
United States of Pussification

We the Pussies of these sassy States,
In order to form a more fussy Union,
Establish Justin Bieber,
Insure domestic timidity,
Provide for a compromised defense,
Promote a continual Welfare State,

And secure diminishing Liberty for ourselves and our
Posterity, do ordain and establish this Constitution for
the United States of Pussification.

Article I – All cultural powers herein granted shall be vested
in the most offended amongst us which shall consist of a Senate,
whatever that is, and a House of Representatives made up of the
man-hating ladies of *The View*.

Article II – The executive power shall be vested in a President
of the United States of Pussification. He shall hold his Office as
long as he doesn't become a Miss-All-That and a bag of potato
chips, and, together with the Vice President, chosen primarily because he's cute and he's not afraid to go postal on Twitter, shall

herein govern our fabulous collective.

Article III – The judicial power of the United States shall be vested in one Supreme Court, comprised of The E! Channel's Fashion Police and Kanye West, and in such inferior Courts as Kanye may from time to time ordain and establish according to his penchants. The judges, both of the supreme and inferior Courts, shall hold their Offices as long as they never listen to that asshat, Doug Giles.

Article IV – Full Faith and Credit shall be given in each State to the National Endowment of the Arts, EMI Records, and the more trendy Proceedings of every other State. And the Congress may by general Laws and stuff prescribe the Manner in which such thingies shall be proved, and the Effect thereof.

Article V – The Congress, whenever two thirds of both Houses think it's like important and all, shall propose Amendments to this Constitution, just as long as it doesn't ruin everything that we created.

Article VI – All Debts contracted and Engagements entered into, before the Adoption of this Constitution, shall not be valid against the United States of Pussification because that hurts our fragile Constitution, and should be deemed judgmental and not applicable because it's just so gross.

Article VII – The Ratification of the Conventions of these various States of Pussification shall be good enough for the Establishment of this Constitution between the States so ratifying the Same. So ... Enjoy.

Chapter 10

Psalm 666:
The State is
My Shepherd

Psalm 666: The State is My Shepherd

Do y'all like poetry? Here's the pussy's favorite poem.

The State is my shepherd, I shall not want.

It makes me lie down in federally owned pastures.

It leads me beside quiet waters in banned fishing areas.

It restores my soul through its control.

It guides me in the path of dependency for its namesake.

Even though our nation plunges into the valley of the shadow of debt, I will fear no evil; for The State will be with me.

The Affordable Care Act and food stamps, they comfort me.

You prepare a table of Michelle Obama-approved foods before me in the presence of my Conservative and Libertarian enemies.

You anoint my head with hemp oil; my government-regulated, 16-ounce cup overflows.

Surely mediocrity and an entitlement mentality will follow me all the days of my life, and I will dwell in a low-rent HUD home forever and ever.

Amen.

Section Four

Of Mice and Pussies

Chapter 11

Dear Christian:
You might be a pussy...
but Jesus ain't

Dear Christian: You Might Be a Pussy...
But Jesus Ain't

When the misinformed thinks of Jesus nowadays, one imagines ...

1. An overly ebullient, grinning hick with a curly mullet, a man bag and a quaint southern drawl, who spits out more aphorisms than Joel Osteen on crystal-meth-laced Mountain Dew.

2. Or The Nazarene gets painted as some rambling, Rasputin-like mystic who strings together long, illogical stories like an unshorn, Bruce-Banner--inspired, Matthew McConaughey grad speech.

3. Either that or Jesus Christo gets pitched as some unisexual, religious, gluten-free Gucci model who might confuse us in regards to his actual gender, but he's crystal clear with his message that we should all be tolerant of the ridiculous no matter how much it offends reason.

Two things are for certain in our culture's postmodern paranormal messaging regarding Christ and Christians:

1. Jesus is not masculine and ...

2. Christianity is for pussies

Indeed, our pussified culture has created for themselves a pussified, Faux Christ, who's nicer than the actual Jesus and has little to nothing to do with the rebellious, young Galilean who kicked up dust on the mean streets in the Middle East many moons ago. Consequently, his followers are expected to produce gelded disciples who do not upset the world like the first century believers did.

Well, as you can imagine, Dear Crispin, I'm here to blow that nonsense all to hell.

The real Jesus of the Scripture was a very hard act to follow. I hate to disparage The Duke, but the Christ of the Bible makes John Wayne look lame.

Jesus was the epitome of a man's man.

Yep, the Jesus of the Scripture razed hell, drank and made wine, was a carpenter before Home Depot and power tools, fashioned a whip and turned over the book tables of the religious dandies of his day, bashed false prophets and wicked politicos and sacrificially gave up his life as a ransom for many. To make that Man into Jared Leto, as far as I'm concerned, is the sin of sins.

If you need proof that I'm not a bubble off level, then grab your journal and hold on to your lug nuts; it's time for an overhaul.

Check out these observations of the Rowdy Christ in the Book of Matthew.

Matthew 2.

- Baby Jesus terrified King Herod so much he tried to kill him.

Matthew 4.

- Jesus kicked Satan's backside on an empty stomach after forty days of fasting.

- Jesus told his followers to quit their jobs and join his revolt. Then he gave them power over frickin' demons. That sounds more exciting than a pussy's life, doesn't it?

Matthew 5-7.

- The famous Sermon On the Mount purposely offended the religious dweebs of his day. It was bold, politically incorrect yumminess, on steroids.

Matthew 8.

- Jesus wasn't some insecure, lame fame-seeker who had to hang out with the *Charisma* magazine's Playmate of the Month. Jesus hung out with riff-raff.

- Jesus was tough on his followers and wouldn't even allow one to bury his own dead dad.

- Jesus didn't shriek like a chick when faced with Cat 5 hurricanes or the worst demon possessed lunatics on the planet.

- Jesus was so dangerous to be around and so controversial, people wanted nothing to do with him.

Matthew 9.

- Jesus purposely went out of his way to mess with self-righteous religious donkeys.

- When Jesus performed a miracle he told the crowd not to tell anyone. A pussy would never do that. No, rather they would build a blog, a Facebook page, and start doing speaking tours to gullible churches that like to hear stories about the time you laid hands on your house cat and he miraculously coughed up the hairball he was choking on.

- Jesus was able to see potential in the worst possible people and places. That's something a shortsighted, fear-laden, visionless pussy would never do.

Matthew 10.

- Jesus gave away the power he had to his boys. That's definitely not something an insecure pastor would ever do.

- Jesus didn't coddle his disciples. He didn't give them any money and he sent them out like sheep to the wolves, in a summit or plummet mission. Since he wasn't a pussy... he made certain that his amigos weren't pussies either.

- Jesus told everyone in earshot of him that he didn't come to bring peace but a sword. He warned his audience that if you follow him you had better expect the crap to hit the fan.

Matthew 11.

- Jesus "commanded" his disciples. Please note: he didn't softly suggest for them to try the Father's way. No… he commanded them.

- Jesus let his buddy John the Baptist go to jail and he didn't try to get him out in any form or fashion. Jesus' buddies weren't little daisies. They did jail time. Have you?

- Jesus said only the "violent enter the Kingdom of Heaven". When's the last time you heard that preached at your "I'm A Daisy Community Church"?

- Jesus berated an apathetic and persnickety generation.

- Jesus condemned to hell entire cities. He pronounced curses upon everyone in the town.

- Jesus said the wise and learned religious know-it-alls wouldn't make it to heaven but only the bruised and broken.

Matthew 12.

- Jesus purposely offended the ridiculous religious rules of his day by eating bread and healing peeps on the Sabbath.

- Jesus was a smart aleck. He asked the wise and the learned of the Scripture, "Have you not read?" when he knew fully well they had read the Scripture. They memorized the first five books of the Bible.

- Jesus so jacked with the religious leaders that they sought to kill him.

- Jesus wasn't interested in the pretty crowds. Yep, he favored the kind of people you wouldn't want to share your Facebook profile picture with.

- Jesus once again told those whom he did great things for to tell no one what he did. In other words, he wasn't some fame-seeking religious whore.

- Jesus was so raw and obtuse towards the religious dandies they nicknamed him *el Diablo*.

- Jesus slapped the label "evil snakes" on the top religious big dawgs of his day.

- Jesus defied his own parents. Yep, Jesus did not obey the sweet Virgin Mary.

Matthew 13.

- Jesus purposefully obscured his messages so that people who thought they had God figured out ended up going to an eternal hell. A squishy pastor would've told the self-righteous, religious hoity-toities that they're God's special people and they're all going to heaven to eat ice cream with Jesus.

Matthew 14.

- Jesus walked on water. Now that, my friend, is some ballsy stuff. I had a buddy we nicknamed "Itchy" who tried to walk on water once after he got all liquored-up at Buffalo Lake back in the early '80's. It was late and we were partying out in the middle of the lake and we dared him to try; and he, like Saint Peter, went for it; and like *San Pedro* he sunk like most men's wedding tackle does when they watch Michelle Obama dance.

- Jesus had so much power radiating off his person that if

you touched his clothes you'd get healed. Pussies don't have that kind of moxie radiating off their skinny jeans. The only thing you'll get if you touch a metrosexual's clothing is the transference of their cheap, unisex perfume they bought just because Justin Bieber wore it once and they somehow think that wearing his *eau de toilette* will morph them into that dork.

Matthew 15.

- Jesus called a lady a dog. A people-pleasing pastor would never call some needy chick a dog to get a point across, but Jesus did. By the way, the lady he dissed wasn't an easily offended Nancy who ran off and filed a defamation of character lawsuit. No, she played his insult/test right and ended up receiving a mega-blessing for her whacked out daughter. See, when Jesus says something offensive, it's best to roll with his punches because most of the time, my little kiddies... he's testing you to see if you're going to pout and die or rise up and live.

Matthew 16.

- Jesus predicted his death and didn't have a pity party about it. He knew what was coming down the pike and that it was going to get rough. Like, in real rough.

- When Peter rebuked Jesus and tried to save his life, Jesus lit him up, called him Satan, and forthrightly proceeded towards his own crucifixion. Most squishy pastors, if they got wind of their death, would hire Blackwater to guard them 24/7. Jesus didn't. He embraced death. He said his death was a must. His death was God's will and he embraced his fate like a man. Tell me that ain't bad-ass.

Matthew 17.

- Jesus rebuked his boys' inability to cast out a wicked demon that kept tossing a kid he possessed into fire and water. He didn't tell his feckless followers, "Well, you did your best." He said, "How long do I have to put up with you? You're perverted and unbelieving." Essentially, he told 'em they hadn't learned a thing after hanging out with him for three years. Question: does that fit your Sweet Jesus image that your church pawned off on you for the last twenty-years? No? I didn't think so.

Matthew 18.

- Jesus said God's kingdom belongs to peeps with kid-like faith, not smarmy, religious jackanapes.

- Jesus said, if you mess with kids, you're dead meat to him at the judgment seat.

- Jesus said he's happier when really messed up sinners come to God than all the squeaky-clean dullards singing "Kumbayah" *ad nauseam, ad infinitum*, at Light-A-Fart Community Church.

- Jesus said to kick someone out of church if they stubbornly persist in their sin. I know ministers who embrace some of the most scurrilous scalawags who don't give two flips about living for God simply because they give mega-money to ministry. Can you say "pussy"? Jesus would never do that. A greedy religious punk would. But not Jesus.

- Jesus also said, if someone's truly sorry for the bad they've done to you, no matter how many times they screw up, that you'd better chill and forgive them or God won't forgive you. Ouch.

Matthew 19.

- Jesus said that anyone who divorces his wife, except for sexual immorality, and marries another woman commits adultery. Boom. You'll hear very few little darlings preach that on Sundays in our divorce-laden "Churches". Hello, pussies!

- Jesus said it's tough for rich people to enter the kingdom of Heaven. He compared it to a camel crawling through the eye of a little needle. In our context, it would be like getting Rosie O'Donnell to squeeze into a size-one catsuit.

Matthew 20.

- Jesus told his goofy disciples, who were wanting to be "rulers", that only sacrificial servants are his true buddies and that's what he considers a real leader.

- Jesus showed compassion, a masculine quality, on people who were truly suffering. He didn't blow them off like selfish, religious douches do.

Matthew 21.

- Jesus kicked some ass in the Temple, driving out all of the religious hucksters who had turned a place of prayer into a place to make lots of money by selling Christian kitsch to sincere religious folks. Doesn't that sound familiar? Can you imagine what would happen if Jesus got air dropped into the 21st Century and personally saw the nasty money machines both Catholic and Protestant churches have morphed into? Shoot… he'd be so personally worn out from kicking so much shyster keister that he'd have to hire massive, multi-member Church Ass-Kicking Squads to go around the country flippin' over cheesy Christian book, CD and DVD display tables at various churches and Christian conferences. I also think Jesus would come real close to cussin' if somehow he were also forced to sit through The Dove Awards, which sports supposed "Christian" talent more shady than The Black Forest.

- Jesus cursed a fig tree and it croaked. Yep, Jesus killed a tree. So much for Jesus being what the liberals depict him as, namely, a doe-eyed tree-hugger. When's the last time your pastor cursed and killed a tree? Never? That's what I thought.

Matthew 22.

- Jesus reduced the law of God down into two simple commands and neither of them has anything to do with not smoking cigars or not drinking beer. Jesus said, "'Love the Lord your God with all your heart and with all your soul and with all your mind" and "Love your neighbor as yourself." Pretty succinct, eh?

Matthew 23.

- Jesus went postal on the nefarious religious leaders of his day, in the most epic smack down ever recorded in the entirety of Scripture. It was a public rebuke that was anything but sweet. He verbally dropped kicked them into next week; exposing their hypocrisy and abuses and pronounced seven curses on their pretty, little, religious heads. Truly awesome, terrifying denunciations delivered by a Christ who had gotten fed up with their crap. It's a must read. Especially in light of the fact that most churches will never preach on them because they're so rough and Christianettes don't like hard sayings... they love only to have their souls stroked on Sunday.

Matthew 24.

- Jesus really goes rogue in this chapter and pronounces some pretty hefty maledictions against impenitent, religious crowds. Yep, in chapter twenty-four Jesus says not only are the people in deep kimchi, but the very Temple is now doomed. By the way, it was no easier in Jesus' day to be politically incorrect than it is in ours.

Matthew 25.

- Jesus unfurls one of the scariest stories I've ever read, called "The Sheep & The Goats". I dare you to read it. It definitely is not for pussies. It'll terrify you but... at the same time... it could save you.

Matthew 26.

- Jesus, on the night of his death, doesn't call the suicide hotline. He doesn't start screaming, "I want my Virgin Mary!" Instead, he has his last meal with his boys and then goes off to pray that God'll give him strength to receive the substitutionary death penalty placed upon his sinless, sacrificial body for our shady ways. And that, my friends, is something no pussy I know would ever do.

- Jesus went to jail and he didn't squeal about it. Oh, and by the way, they abused him in prison and yet he didn't cry, freak or scream. That's dude stuff, Crispin.

- Jesus lost all of his friends and he still plowed on and did what he had to do even though it was the most difficult thing any human being has ever done.

Matthew 27.

- Jesus stood before the governor, who could've let him go, and instead held his ground, stuck to what he knew to be true; which lead to a beating no pussy could stand thirty seconds of.

- Finally, Jesus was executed and it wasn't for any crime he had committed and it was about as unpleasant an execution that demented minds could imagine... a crucifixion.

Matthew 28.

- Jesus, after three days in the grave, rises from the dead. That, my friends, is the definition of defiant bad-assedness. Death was not going to hold him down. Can you say... boom?

- Jesus, after three days gone, decided to go mountain climbing with his buddies and then tells their fear-laden backsides to cheer up, he now has all authority, and now go... and change the world... teach the planet everything that I commanded you.

And that, my friends, is a feat that no pussy could ever accomplish; but Jesus did.

Now, do you still want to believe the blather that Jesus was lame and Christianity is for pussies?

Matter of fact, if you want to be a real man, then follow The Man from Galilee.

My cigar
smells yucky?

Not as bad as
your mangina does.

~Doug Giles

Chapter 12

Business Owners Should Avoid Pussies Like the Plague

Business Owners Should Avoid
Pussies Like the Plague

I don't know a business owner schlepping this rock, who has a company that he wants to succeed, who would knowingly hire... a pussy.

For certain, some do hire pussies for various stupid and regretful reasons. However, if they could, in a perfect world, most would avoid employing a man-child like Trump would flee from a Wet T-Shirt Contest featuring Rosie O'Donnell and her pasty and droopy stalactites and her gelatinous, bulbous gut.

Further, I don't know any individuals that want to dole out their hard earned cash and purposely contract out some dilatory dolt to do any job, big or small.

Yea, dear reader, when it comes down to handling a company's goods, services or merchandise I know of no one with a lick of sense who will say to themselves, "Hey, self, why don't you hire a pussy for this task?"

But, for whatever reason, sadly, we do; and the ubiquitous dandies do slip into our employ.

My purpose for this chapter is to help business owners avoid pussies like the plague. I hope this chapter helps you to quickly spot them and get rid of them PDQ before they cost you your time, talent and treasure.

In addition to doing the aforementioned, I also intend to give you, little Crispin, some advice on how not to be smoke in the eyes of your employer. And with that opening salvo, let's have some fun, shall we?

First off, allow me to bash some of us who have ever hired a pussy. Yep, before I go postal on the pussies, we need to take it on the chin and own up to the fact that it's usually our fault if we ever got sideswiped by a douche that we employed when we shouldn't have.

Here's what I mean:

> Pussies will eat away at your financial bottom line.

For example: Did you really have to hire your dorky relative to work for your company? Really? Because, I'm a-guessin', if they weren't your kin you probably wouldn't have paid them a plugged nickel to rake dog crap in your kennel because they're so inept.

Look, nobody forced you to do that, but you "wanted to help the family", so you did; and now you're suffering the negative consequences, which I will discuss later, by hiring a limp biscuit "just because they had your last name or your mother's maiden name"; or were somehow roughly connected to your gene pool, which, evidently, someone must have peed in at one time or the other. But I digress.

In addition, did you really do due diligence in your hiring process? Did you truly perform a serious background check? Were you so desperate to hire whomever that desperation overrode intelligence and intuition and now you're in a SNAFU of ginormous proportions?

Look, we've all done it.

What we must do, going forward, is mitigate the likelihood of that self-inflicted gunshot wound to the wallet ever occurring again.

Before I plow on allow me to allay any angst you might have in being a hard-ass in the judging and hiring process for your business, which is, by the way, your baby. Speaking of babies, just like you wouldn't allow Achmed the Dead Terrorist to babysit your little daughter, you should be equally reticent to allow a dipstick into your company's ranks.

Here's why you shouldn't "feel bad" or that "you're being mean" by not giving a googin a shot and a spot in your company. Are ready?

One great reason why you should not hire the lame is… God warns you not to.

> Do a serious background check before hiring.

And when God speaks, we should listen because… well… he's God and we're clods and he loves us enough that he doesn't want our gig to get hamstrung by some ham-fisted wanker.

So, don't feel like you're unrighteously being difficult because even God loathes and warns us away from employing *lé pussy*.

"Where doth God warn me away from the soul-sucking saps that'll zap the life out of my company?" you asked?

Well, I'm glad you asked, you inquiring mind you. It's in King Solomon's bag of goodies, the Book of Proverbs.

Oh, by the way, and this one's for free: if you're some whiny, supposed "atheist" twit who just recoiled at my mentioning God and the Bible, and you're "so offended" now that you're not going to continue to read or listen to what I have to say, then I have four words for you:

Are you ready?

Here they are:

YOU.

ARE.

A.

PUSSY.

How's that?

Do you mean to tell me and others, with a straight face, that you can't consider a staid piece of respected literature and not feel threatened? Wow. Aren't you special? You should run for Prom Queen of Pussville High School. Or better yet, we should anoint you the Princess of Little Bitch Mountain. Now, where was I? Oh, yeah …

For certain, Solomon doesn't label the pussies "pussies" in his inspired denunciations. He calls them "sluggards" which is a major character trait/flaw of the overcooled that I'm clobbering.

And please note: to be called a sluggard is in no way less than being called a pussy. So don't think that's a non-offensive moniker, because it is; and no one who has a stitch of pride would ever want that flag to be flown over their castle. Indeed, pussy and sluggard, as far as I'm concerned,

> **Even God warns against hiring pussies. Take heed.**

and that's all that matters, are the same damn thing. And I mean "damn" in the biblical sense of the word, meaning… accursed. Because what the sluggard brings to your company, as you will see, is anything but… a blessing.

Without further ado, here's what the wisest man in the world has to say about the sluggard, how to spot them and why a business owner must avoid them. I guarantee you've never heard your Hipster, skinny- jeaned pastor ever hammer his shiftless congregation with these goodies.

1. The sluggard is a lazy.

> "How long will you lie there, you sluggard? When will you get up from your sleep? A little sleep, a little slumber, a little folding of the hands to rest—and poverty will come on you like a thief and scarcity like an armed man."

> Proverbs 6:9-11 (NIV)

Dear Bosses: did you catch what the lazy-ass sluggard attracts to himself? Poverty and scarcity. Question: is that what you want for your company? Poverty and scarcity?

Huh? Do you want your business to be impoverished? If so... then hire someone who's lazy. Hire a procrastinator. Hire someone who's attached to their bed. Hire the laggard who's apathetic, dull, inattentive, indifferent, passive, comatose, inert, lymphatic, moony, nebbishy and languorous; and you can kiss your sweet profits, *adios*!

2. The sluggard is an excuse-maker.

A sluggard says,

"There's a lion in the road, a fierce lion roaming the streets!"

Proverbs 26:13 (NIV)

One thing a pussy is really good at is making excuses for why he's unable to fulfill the duty he's been paid to do. When Solomon penned the aforementioned golden nugget, Israel still held a decent population of lions. So, the ancient pussy, hiding his ancient pussiness, brought up the reality of man-eaters being in proximity to his person as an excuse to why he "can't" work today. Pretty creative, eh? "I can't work because a lion might eat me." Well, kiss my grits.

Business owners, you know that the business world is fraught with "lions" that love to eat workers and the companies they work for. It's par for the course. It's the law of the jungle. Eat or be eaten. The business world is bloody. It's war. And the bigger the business, the bloodier. Therefore, if you have in your employment someone who

> King Solomon said "Don't hire pussies!" AKA sluggards.

keeps whining about competition or how difficult things are in the "Serengeti" wherein you labor, then you have an excuse-making pussy on your hands that you need to cut because the more they yarble about lions the more they cudgel off your growth and profits. Also, here's a little FYI: their excuse-making spirit will spread like wild fire and infect your entire company. So... can them, asap.

3. The sluggard is a taxing bastard.

"Go to the ant, O sluggard, Observe her ways and be wise, Which, having no chief, Officer or ruler, Prepares her food in the summer And gathers her provision in the harvest."

Proverbs 6:6-8 (NIV)

Solomon implies, in Proverbs Six, that the sluggard needs a boss or they won't do jack. I call those types of pussies "wheel barrow people." They only go as far as you push them and that's it. Your best bet is to get rid of people who require constant supervision and prodding. They're stubborn jackasses and you can't make a racehorse out of a jackass.

> Pussies have a lazy work ethic.

Oh, I'm sure some of you employers think you're like Jesus and can turn water into wine, but you'll find out soon enough that if they aren't internally motivated you're not going to change them; and if you keep them in your company you'll end up screwed, glued and tattooed. What you're hunting for in an employee is the ant-like dude or dudette that doesn't need a boss's constant whip crackin' over them in order to get stuff done.

4. The sluggard craves.

"The soul of the sluggard craves and gets nothing."

Proverbs 13:4 (NIV)

This is an interesting little ditty about the pussy, and one that employers often get bamboozled by, namely, the sluggard craves. Yep, the dilatory do have desires. They want to live like Puff Daddy. They want the nice house, the sweet ride and the cool vacations, but they won't do diddlysquat to righteously attain what they dream about on mamma's couch, doing bong hits, while masturbating to the *Price Is Right*'s spokesmodels.

To listen to them blather about what they want and where they would like to be, oftentimes, can be confused with ambition when, in reality, it's a frickin' pipe dream. It's as unreal as an acid trip.

In my fifty-three years I've heard these dreamy clowns talk about who they want to be and where they want to go, but at the end of the day, they sit on their butts and do little to nothing to attain what they crave. Your best bet is, after you hear them yodel about wanting to be the next Bon Jovi, check to see if they have a great track record of working their butt off. If not, you've got a dreamy pussy on your hands.

5. The sluggard is arrogant.

"The sluggard is wiser in his own eyes than seven men who can give a discreet answer."

Proverbs 26:16 (NIV)

I love this one. The pussy, who hasn't done anything in life, thinks he's smarter than the accomplished.

In July of 2012, my business partner and I launched our political blog, ClashDaily.com. At this writing, June 2016, we've had 150 million page views, built a Facebook fan base of 570,000 with a weekly reach, via Facebook, of three-to-four million. That's not too shabby. The funny thing is that, during our inception and along our merry way, we've had a stack of clowns tell us "we could do what you're doing better than you're doing it."

> Pussies need constant supervision or they won't work.

The fact I find entertaining is they haven't; and we're still crushing it. But, if one were to listen to them, they would crow with great unction that they're "way more savvy than Team Clash". But there they are, doing nada except pulling lint out of their navel while we stomp skulls.

Please note: Pussies love… and I mean love… to tell themselves, their mother, their three cats and their clueless wife and/or girlfriend who's paying their bills, that they're the sharpest knife in the drawer. But they're not. They're nothing but a dreamy lot of hot air. Therefore, don't let their delusions deter you or shock you when you hear these carpy, lardy hagfish try to upstage you. They're wise, according to Solomon, only in their eyes and are; by their very nature, "fools" whose endgame is a crappy life, followed by destruction (Proverbs 24:30, 34; 6:11).

As you can tell, a myopic cyclops can see why Solomon shoos the shrewd business owner away from the half-cocked, fully baked pussy. Who the heck wants a wafty, unmotivated, excuse making, know-it-all, who lives for comfort over duty, anywhere near their enterprise? The answer: no one who has a scintilla of common sense, that's who.

> Pussies are entitlement people. They want it all for nothing.

Finally, here's some advice for you, little Crispin, if you wish to thrive in a competitive world and move up the ladder of success, versus being a government-handout stooge of the machine. So... pull out your journal and jot down these twenty bullet points.

In the event that you actually do have a job, or wish to one day have one, do the following:

- Show up on time.

- Stay off social media unless your job is social media, you ass-clown.

- Don't call in sick unless you have Ebola.

- Don't waste your company's money.

- Make your company as much money as possible.

- Always think about how you can better the company.

- Look sharp. Don't pierce your tongue unless you work in the porn industry. And if you are a porn star, make sure you have a great life insurance policy for your loved ones because you're gonna die a horrible death soon. Also, if you work at a gym try to be in shape. No one's going to believe Gold's Gym is great if you can hide small toys in the folds of your fat. Also, unless you're the High Priest of the Church of Satan, or the lead singer of Godsmack, or a killer tattoo artist, or a custom chopper maker, I'd really think long and hard about getting your neck and face tatted up, unless you're cool with being a barista for the rest of your life at Starbucks.

- Understand that there are only two jobs that start on top: And that's grave digging and well digging. Everything thing else entails your starting at the bottom. If you ever want to sit on the throne you must start by cleaning the toilets.

- Be dependable. Become known for being "Johnny on the Spot".

- Sport a great attitude. Nobody likes a sad clown.

- Become multi-skilled. The more things you can master, the fatter your wallet will become.

> **Pussies think they know it all.**
>
> ...
>
> **But they don't.**

- Be pro-active. If something is jacked up, fix it.

- Finish what you start.

- Crank up your communication skills and try to learn to speak like an adult instead of a douche.

- Learn how to adapt and be creative with your job.

- Manage yourself instead of constantly needing a babysitter to make sure you haven't crapped your diaper.

- Don't be a self-obsessed me-monkey.

- Don't make ease your chief end.

- Embrace sacrifice, sweat and pain.

- Finally, treat your employer with respect because, if it weren't for him, you'd be eating government cheese and living in a van down by the river.

Your job
is hard?

Imagine being
Hillary Clinton's
bikini-waxer.

~Doug Giles

Chapter 13

Real Women
Hate Pussies

Real Women Hate Pussies

"How do you know what a woman wants?" I can hear the lesbians, I mean feminists, screech at this chapter's title.

Well, truth be told. I know *nada* about what women want except the fact that there are very few things in life that a flat iron and a bottle of wine can't cure.

Look, I'll own it. I'm not a Chick Whisperer. I got no dawg in that hunt. After twenty-eight great years of marriage and raising two gorgeous girls, women are still a lovely mystery me. And I'm cool with that.

One thing I do know for certain, about Italian women at least, is: if they're hungry do not, under any circumstances, piss them off.

That said, my wife and I have spent the better part of a quarter century ministering to males and females, from all over the world, and one thing I've heard from women of all races, colors and creeds is… they hate men who're pussies.

Maybe hate is too strong of a word.

Correction, they like and befriend males who're pussies. They enjoy going shopping with them and sharing gossip and Frappuccinos. However, when it comes to hitching their wagon, spitting out some babies and walking into a room of peeps they're looking to impress, schlepping with a dandy does not even raise a blip on their radar. The sad thing is that women outnumber men and young men, who would be men, are about as hard to find as 40" markhor is in a West Texas cotton field. Good luck, ladies.

Yep, I feel sorry for the young single women out there.

Sure, it's your day and "the sky's the limit" when it comes to career possibilities and voting and crap. But when it comes to your options of viable single young men to date and eventually marry, the only thing that seems "limitless" on your bleak horizon are pussies aplenty. Sure there are tons of young males to choose from, but there's only a smattering of young men.

> Real women "friend" pussies but they "love" men.

I blame four things for this massive nutless/gutless glut: 1. Pop culture; 2. Public schools; 3. Sassy branches of Catholicism and Protestantism; 4. Homes without an awesome dad.

Allow me to explain.

Pop culture has made softy, man-bun-sporting pukes the norm. Public schools have shamed and drugged natural masculine traits from boys. The Church has hard-peddled a soft-focused bearded lady version of Jesus who's more akin to a liberal Austin hippie than the rebellious Christ of the Bible. And women have bought into Hollywood's horsehockey, lock stock and two smokin' barrels, that ladies can raise kids without the input of a masculine man in the house. These four lethal ingredients have created a perfect storm for the proliferation of pussies galore. No wonder lesbianism is all the rage. At least you can exchange clothes and make up. Wait, I take that back. Metrosexuals now wear make-up. My bad.

Questioning my jaded judgment regarding women and their slim pickens when it comes to dudes, I turned to Facebook and posed this question to the *chicas*:

"DEAR LADIES: Do you like traditional, old-school, manly

men or effeminate, metrosexual males? What you put here is going to go into my book, *PUSSIFICATION* (with anonymity, of course). If you would, please, give a good, but brief, explanation."

Here's the girls' response:

Angelina- I love manly alpha men. Nothing is worse than seeing a liberal man following a femiNasty around Trader Joe's and she's got his balls in her purse.

Laura - Gimme extra testosterone for my hairy platter of lumberjack arms and chest.

Jan - I like a strong man. That is not afraid to SPEAK up for what is right. Not like the wussssss in White House. There is lots of sexy on a strong Alpha male. That can express himself and what he likes...if ya know what I mean. Lol. But most important is a God fearing man. Nothing more strong than a man not afraid to admit he needs God in his life to lead.

> **Real women want men who lead.**

Lisa - I'll take a pick-up-truck-driving, cigar-smoking, whiskey-drinking, God-fearing, gun-toting, scruffy-faced alpha male any day...bonus points if he can cook what he kills.

Lori - I definitely want a manly man who is in tune with himself and with me. He knows his wants and needs and he knows my needs, and we work together to satisfy those needs, wants, in each other.

Mary - Traditional. I had the other for 18 years of marriage. After 5 kids (all girls) I wised up and got divorced. He was narcissistic, loved his mommy and was addicted to porn. I now have that traditional old school manly man and sometimes cannot believe the difference-it's AMAZING!

Lori - I've been there too, still waiting for my traditional man to come along and if he doesn't, I'll stay single. I will NOT settle again!

Suzanne - Manly man please. One who can protect his family, armed if necessary, provide for his family, honor his wife and knows how and when to speak up for what is right. Affection is good, whiny, needy jerks aren't. Belittling others... not attractive. Using more skin products than I do? Oh hell no! Suck it up and be a man.

Megan - Will any woman admit an attraction to Pajama Boy? I just don't even think women who are with men like that are attracted to them...they just like the fact that there's someone they can boss around

Johannah - If he takes longer to get ready than I do... We have a problem! I will also add; if your boyfriend takes more selfies than you do, you both need to see other men.

> Real women like men with an extra side of testosterone.

Clarissa - Manly man with pants that fit. I'm also so tired of seeing these so called men walking around with their man purses. Love my hubby of almost 10 years and all his manly ways including holding the door open for me.

Lana - I prefer a strong man (I finally got one!) and love being accepted for who I am, slightly crazy with what hubby calls, "That Italian gene!"

I will make him as happy I can and look after his health because I prayed so hard for a real man and waited 30 years

Jessica- Manly man if I would have wanted the other I would have been lesbian!

Jo Ann - What good is an effeminate man to a woman except to be a sister she never had!

Kimberly - I can't handle a guy who: doesn't play and/or like sports, who likes cats over dogs, who is a male school teacher and the only sport he likes is bowling, who is afraid of horses, who is a liberal, who cries.

Ashley - I prefer and Have a real man! A man who works hard and doesn't complain, works through sickness and pain. Believes in physical labor when it comes to disciplining kids, plus a whooping. Likes Cigars and whiskey haha! Wears clothes that fit, has a beard

Maria- I like a man to be a gentleman and A woman to be ladies.

Staci - Totally a manly man. A warrior! I can be tough and was that for almost 40 years. But I wanted someone who loved, honored and protected me to give me the safety to be soft and feminine to the core. I don't have to worry about looking over my shoulder

Kami - I need a real man. Skinny jeans are proven to cut off circulation to their brains. And the only good thing about man buns is that they provide secret room to hide your tampons. Give me gunpowder and lead any day of the week and twice on Sunday.

Meredith - how many expletives am i allowed? LOL!

From the replies my query garnered it looks like I was right... again.

Now, heretofore, in this soon to be best-selling book, I've been directly addressing the ubiquitous and gelded "Crispins" that populate our unfortunate planet, trying to move them successfully from Pussville into the rarified air of Mantown. But for now, allow me, fair lasses, a reprieve to speak to you for one thousand words or so because you might very well be dating a pussy and not know it.

> Real women like chivalry. It's not dead, just under-used.

Here's five tell-tale signs. Take notes, please.

1.   A pussy won't open the door for you.

Unless you're going into a demon possessed house or a room that could possibly be booby trapped by Islamic terrorists, a real man will open the door for you like you're something special because -- you know what? -- you are. And that's one way he shows he values you over him. A true young gentleman gets that. I'll never forget watching this couple prior to their marriage. Every time they'd come over to the house or rock up to an event, the guy would always be blowing through the door with his girlfriend in tow with the now-closing door hitting her in the face. Later, after their nuptials and after they had a stack of kids, he still did the same thing. He'd careen into the venue like Kramer and she'd be left fending for the babies, draggin' car seats and strollers, all the while he's footloose and fancy free. I finally had to rebuke him saying, "Dude ... help your frickin' wife."

>   2. A pussy won't walk with you down a street and stay between you and the curb.

Here's an FYI that's going to carbon-date me back to T-Rex's era: A gentleman always walks closest to the curb. The curb is where danger dwells. Especially in this day of texting jackasses and drunk drivers. The reason is simple: If someone's gonna die or be injured or drenched by some yucky-ass curb water, then let it be you, you dolt. For the feral young males who were raised after the age of chivalry, the right side is the honorary side. A man will have the woman walk on his right side.

It's called, etiquette. It's how a real man says, in a practical way, "I honor you". This masculine trait dates back to the middle ages, when knights wore their sword on the left side, keeping the right side free to beat some ass while the lady would always walk on the "protected side".

> **If men and women are identical, then one gender is unnecessary.**

>   3. A pussy can't find his way around a killer restaurant.

First off, you can forget about *el dipstick* chasing down a special place to eat and making the reservations, because he has used up all his strength and brainpower plucking his eyebrows and trying to perfect Kim Kardashian's pout. A gentleman, on the other hand, takes the initiative, hunts down a great establishment and makes the reservation. A Metrosexual will tag along versus taking the lead, you see. So, wherever you and your girlfriends decide you're going to dine, that's where that puss of a boyfriend of yours is going to go. A man, on the other hand, not only will make the reservation, but will make friends with the owner, and bribe the hostess for a great table. Also, if your male doesn't rise when you enter the room, help you be seated and give you his jacket if it gets cold, then guess what you got *señorita*? You got yourself a selfish pussy.

4. A pussy won't pay for dinner.

My wife and I listened in horror a couple of weeks ago when an acquaintance of ours started raggin' about her boyfriend regarding how he never pays for dinner dates or they go Dutch. As soon as she finished speaking, I told her without hesitation, to dump his sorry ass now because it just gets worse. Girls ... if you're paying for food and/or drinks when you're with "your man"... then, FYI, you don't have a man. You have a scum-sucking parasite that's glammed onto your bank account. That's what you got, sister. That, m'lady, is anything but a man; and if you continue to let this leech French kiss you, then I hope you're ready to work your ass off after he fathers two to four kids through your vagina be-cause he ain't gonna change. He won't pay for diddly. By the way, dating is the test to show whether that sack of crap sitting across the table from you is going to pro-vide. Jesus said a man's money is where his

> Real women like men who are polite.

heart is, and if he's not dropping coin on you then his heart's not in it and you'd better wake the hell up, Sleeping Beauty. If you think I'm full of crap, then plow on, but remember... you've... been... warned. Oh, and while I'm at it, a pussy is never on time, won't say, "please" and "thank you", will not mind his table manners, is rude to servers and will not get you safely home.

5. A pussy won't ask for your family's blessing in marriage.

> Real women like men with a protective instinct.

Especially, if you have an Alpha Dad. Here's why: Daddy Warbucks sends out a Tarzan vibe ten miles wide and high and he, more than likely, can see right through your unaccomplished, shady and shiftless, veil of crap, that your prancing little Dandy of a beau lives behind. And that scares the bejesus out of him. If you're dating a Hello Kitty, and you've got a functional family that loves you deeply, and your Puss-N-Boots boyfriend will not honorably face the people who love and care for you more than life itself and ask for their blessing on your betrothal, then you need to run from him like Bill does Hillary when she's in one of her "moods". Here's the deal: Good dads adore their daughters. They love them unconditionally and without reserve. They have raised them and have provided for them to the best of their ability and have prayed for a great young man to come along who'll love, honor and cherish the apple of their eye; and your little Rico Suave should do the manly thing and honor that deep tie. If he doesn't, send that scrub packing.

> Real women like to be treated special.

By the way, gents, you can do the aforementioned without becoming a doormat and a mere tortured errand boy to a control-freak chick with a histrionic personality disorder. Also, from what I hear, real women love gentlemen but hate groveling dudes. You can be a gentleman without being a putz. Too nice is too gross. And chivalry doesn't demand a man be grovelly to an abusive chick.

Lastly, ladies, make sure your dude is courageous. A lack of courage is a bad sign. As in, a very bad sign. You want your boyfriend and/or husband to stand for what's right. To be appropriately mouthy and defiant towards inequities and absurdities when they raise their heads, and to try to have a determining influence on bettering public life. Forego the passive dullard who's too caught up in the inconsequential that he does not lead you and others to fight the giants in the land that seek to make our planet suck. If you can find a courageous young man who's got the five bullet points down that I just laid out, then you've got a keeper.

Section Five

Pussies Ain't Easy to Love and They're Harder to Mold

Dear Whiner: You've flown so often to Pussville... you have lifetime platinum status on Bitch-Air.

~Doug Giles

Chapter 14

Mammas Don't Let Your Cowboys Grow up to be Pussies

MAMMAS, DON'T LET YOUR BABIES GROW UP TO BE PUSSIES

Verse 1
Pussies ain't easy to love and they're harder to mold,

They prance 'round in man thongs with lots of diamonds and gold,

 Gucci belt buckles and Ralph Lauren flannels,

And each night starts out very lame.

If you don't understand him, that's simply not his problem,

He'll prob'ly just sashay away.

Chorus
Mammas, don't let your cowboys grow up to be pussies.

Don't let 'em stare at iPads or drink lattes at Starbucks.

 Make 'em be hunters and farmers and such.

Mammas, don't let your cowboys grow up to be pussies.

Cause they'll forever stay home and they'll constantly moan,

 Even with someone they love.

Verse 2
Pussies like steamy, posh spa-rooms and lavender mornings,

 Little warm kitties and Shakira and even Justin Bieber's alright.

Them that don't know him won't like him and them that do

 Sometimes won't know how to take him.

His wiring's all wrong, he's so very gone but his pride won't let him

Do things to make you think he's right.

<u>Chorus</u>
Mammas, don't let your cowboys grow up to be pussies.

Don't let 'em stare at iPads or drink lattes at Starbucks.

Make 'em be hunters and farmers and such.

Mammas, don't let your cowboys grow up to be pussies.

Cause they'll forever stay home and they'll constantly moan

Even with someone they love

Chapter 15

How Fathers Can Avoid Raising a Barack Obama

How Fathers Can Avoid Raising a Barack Obama

I can't think of a more important job than raising your kids right. Don't believe me? Well then, I have two words for you: Michael and Moore.

As much as some stretch-panted lesbian might try to marginalize the role of fathers with their mullet-headed, misguided, misandristic Weltanschauung, the stats clearly state that when pop is in the house, and he properly doles out TLC, the kids come out as a great asset to the planet instead of selfish jackasses.

And that's what our country needs: parents raising hardy kids who love God and our country and don't cost our nation one red cent, but rather add tremendous value to this great experiment in self-governance.

Y'know, sometimes I wonder if Obama had been properly fathered then maybe our country wouldn't be so embarrassed, in debt and internationally laughed at right now.

Therefore, and herewith, are nine ways you, the young dad, can make certain you don't raise a kid like *el presidente*.

1. Make sure your children appreciate this nation, its founding docs and its original intent and not some wet dream Bill Ayers and Bernadine Dohrn had back in the late '60s when

they were high on acid, Che Guevara and Saul Alinsky. Especially be certain that they love our Armed Forces who protect us and not slice and dice their benefits.

2. Make certain your kids know it's wrong to lie your butt off to people who have given you their trust. For instance, if you tell people "they can keep their health care plan and their doctors, period!" then mean that, dammit.

3. If in the event your offspring does make mistakes and situations get worse under their care, train your child to own their mistakes instead of blaming others for their ham-fisted, ill-thought out blunders.

4. Teach your child that glib speeches read from a teleprompter that are laced with platitudes and horse manure do not replace character, honesty and integrity.

5. Lovingly school your young child that when he gets older, writing two books about yourself, or worse yet, having them ghost-written about oneself, is really, *really* weird and doesn't make one a great leader but rather a Little Lord Fauntleroy.

6. Take the time also to train your dear child to throw a baseball properly so he doesn't look ... uh ... um ... effeminate should he ever be called upon to throw out a first pitch during a baseball game.

7. Father, if you have a son, let him know it's okay for him to drink out of a straw when he's like ... uh ... three but not when he's the leader of the free world. At least not in public; and if he ever does drink from a straw in public tell him to never look someone of the same sex in the eye while doing so. The same goes for eating a banana.

8. In addition, dads, please instruct your spawn not to frickin' spy on people. Okay? It's rude and no one likes it and people will think you're a paranoid control freak.

9. And finally, teach your young whippersnapper if he is a boy to forego marrying a mean woman who's ashamed of this nation and wants to police what people eat and don't eat.

Section Six

From Pussville to Mantown

Question: How many accomplished friends do you have?

None? That's why your life sucks, and a big reason why you're a pussy.

~Doug Giles

Chapter 16

Hang Around Bad-Asses

Hang Around Bad-Asses

Check this crap out. According to FOX Carolina in Greenville, South Carolina, Botox is now all the rage for... men?

Yep, the wizards with the American Society of Plastic Surgeons state that the number of dudes getting botulism jacked into their face for vanity reasons jumped ten percent in 2014 to 300,000-plus.

This all too-fussy-for-me trend is called "Brotox."

Isn't that sassy?

Now, why doth aging insecure males inject poison into their noggins?

Well, according to one douche, who did not want to be identified, he said it's because,

> "Nobody likes to look their age. Any man's afraid he's gonna get bumped by somebody younger in business or personal life too. I think once he gets over the stigma of it being something feminine, I could see more men being drawn to it."

And that's why Dr. Sutton Graham's appointment book is filling up with the dandies wanting facial fillers and Botox. "They bring up specifically their employment and how it affects them in their job with their co-workers and with clients and people they meet," Graham said.

One patient said it doesn't take long and it doesn't hurt, "Botox did not hurt at all. It's just a pin prick in your forehead."

Awww. Thank God, it doesn't hurt the wittle sweeties, eh?

Hey, Unidentified Brotox Male: This is Doug Giles and I have a message for you and the fragile, Botox-tempted cabal.

I don't mind looking my age.

Matter of fact, I *like* to look my age, you pussy.

I'm fifty-three years young as I type this best-selling book and I wear my greying hair, my crow's feet and my other attendant wrinkles and scars, brought about by a life well-lived, with righteous pride.

Personally, I think any man who tries to hide nature's natural maturation marks is a wee bit weird.

Also, please note, that Clooney, Mel Gibson and Jeremy Irons, and many others less famous, don't have any problems with getting jobs or chicks because they sport grey follicles and wrinkles. Some companies and lassies like a mature man who brings deep and rich life experiences to enterprises and relationships.

And yes, "Brotox" is "feminine" and no, men should not "get over that."

Oh, and one more thing: people might tell you that "you look great" after getting Brotoxed, but behind the scenes they're laughing their butt off at your frozen features and your scary fastidious obsession with your outward appearance.

That said, I'm all about keeping fit and looking as good as possible, but for God's sake, enough with Brotox and wearing T-Shirts so tight that you confuse the children with your man-tits.

How do I segue way out of that rant into this chapter?

Honestly, Crispin, I don't know how. But that's okay. What I lack in creativity I'm about to make up for in solidly moving you from Pussville into Mantown.

Check it out…

1. Hang Around Bad-Asses.

Question: how many truly bad-ass friends do you have?

I'm talking about people that are accomplished in life... spiritually... physically... mentally... and materially?

None?

Well... there you go, Crispin.

That's why your life sucks and that's a big reason why you're a pussy.

Here's a simple little lesson you should jot down... are you ready?

Do you have your lame journal out?

Because I'm about to delve out some divine wisdom that is worth way more than the cost of this book.

Matter of fact, you should send me a check to my P.O. Box right now for at least $5000 just for this nugget.

Now... are you ready?

You are?

Okay, numbnuts... here we go... you're a pussy because you hang out with pussies and it's just that simple.

Like begets like. Fire begets fire. And pussies beget pussies. Get it? Got it? Good.

Oh... and it gets worse.

Please note: your lame life and your feckless friend choice have probably got you irrevocably screwed.

Like in, forever.

Like in... you'd better hope you're born again because this life is going to suck so bad because of your poor relationship decisions that you'd better know that your soul's saved so at least you're not also burning for all eternity in Dante's Inferno.

Here's another FYI:

Jot this down in your journal as well.

Accomplished people will not want to hang around you, unless you've thoroughly repented from being magna cum mamma's boy and have proven you've been consistent on this radical new path for at least... oh... the last five years.

Check it out.

Those who aren't pussies, like you, aren't looking to befriend pussies because of the likelihood that you'll suck the living daylights out of their life and diffuse their greatness and drag them down to your level of Whiskey Tango Foxtrot.

You must understand this: it will be hard to accomplish the aforementioned and here's why, please pardon my redundancy but, bad-asses aren't looking to sidle up to lame-asses.

I know I sure ain't looking to make friends with a dillweed.

> As iron sharpens iron, so one
> man sharpens another.

However difficult it will be for you to both leave the flock of the rudderless you schlepp with and make new relationships with solid people who'll probably stiff arm you unless you pay them money, the first "must" you must do to decidedly move the hell away from Pussville to Mantown is to get around bad-asses.

Their indomitable spirit will jump off on you.

* PS: Also read biographies of people who went through way worse hell than you ever have or will and pray to God you get a scintilla of their warrior spirit.

* PPS: In addition, fill your house with art that inspires you not to be a Nancy. For instance, in my house I surround myself with my art work, which primarily consists of Africa's Big Five; the grandest and most dangerous critters known to walk God's green globe. I also have portraits of great leaders like King David and Winston Churchill. They feed my spirit. When I start to feel like a timid titmouse, I look at these great men, women and animals, then say to myself, "Self, you're being rather toady today." I then punch myself in the face and then get busy kicking ass versus sit-

ting on my ass. By the way, if you're married and your wife has decorated your house to look like a place where a gutless wonder dwells, then it's time to remodel. If she whines about it... you probably married the wrong chick. Call a lawyer.

Unteachable people usually end up being ...

The High Priest, of the one man cult called, The Church Of I'm An Unteachable Pussy.

~Doug Giles

Chapter 17

Be Teachable

Be Teachable

Another sure-fire way to get the heck out of Pussville and well on your way to Mantown is to shut your blathering pie-hole and listen and obey pretty much everything the bad-asses tell you to do.

Greatness, little Crispin, is not all about standing up to dragons and demons, it's also having the courage to shut the blank up and listen. Capice?

Yes, I said it.

You, the pussy, need to shut the front door and listen.

How many of you have ever opened your mouth when you should've shut up? I know I have. For the first thirty years I had chronic foot in mouth disease. It got so bad my mouth was actually shaped like my foot.

I'll never forget this one time when I learned a hard lesson on shutting up.

One afternoon I was driving my Z28 around and I slow rolled through a stop sign. I didn't flat out run the stop sign… I just didn't come to full stop.

A cop was sitting just off the intersection and busted me breaking the law. When he approached my car he asked me if I knew why he pulled me over and I said no. He said I ran the stop sign. I said no I didn't, that I slowed down and looked both ways before I went through and I saw no real difference between coming to a full stop versus slowing down. The cop said you see no big difference between stopping and slowing down, eh? And I said no. Without missing a beat, he grabbed me through my window, extracted his nightstick and start beating the crap out of me. I start screaming like a little chick, shouting, "What are you doing?" He said, "What... you mean you don't like this? Do you want me to stop or just slow down?"

You see... I should have listened versus saying anything.

Now, I'm sure your mommy has told you ever since you were born that you're just like baby Jesus and that you have a unique talent or gift which precludes you from listening to advice from more accomplished and shrewd mortals.

However, and more than likely, you're nothing like the Son of God and, therefore, you need to zip it and listen to the experts; because you have crap-all to prove that your heretofore wisdom is worth dog scat.

> **Don't mince words. You don't know jack.**

For instance, I know this one dude in Jersey who fancies himself an alpha-dawg. He's hyper-talented and bravado filled. But in regards to truly doing something with the abilities he has, he really hasn't done anything worth writing home about.

The reason why?

Well... simply put ... he's an unteachable jackass; and I use that term in the biblical sense of the word.

No one knows more than he does. And I mean no one. And he'll tell you that he's very close to omniscience and he won't be kidding. He's sold on himself. He actually believes the voices in his head.

The funny thing is that his "brilliance" has never landed him a steady job or a noteworthy accomplishment.

Work wise and relationally, he's burned more bridges than Christopher Haun did during the Civil War and ... and... he still lives at his mommy's house. Awww. Isn't that sweet? Oh, by the way, he's able to do this by telling himself "he's doing it for his mother" but his mamma is very healthy and self-sufficient.

The only thing I can deduce from this male's run of "bad luck" is:

1. Either God hates him or...

2. He's a pussy who hides behind bluster and some talent and is not open to be taught diddlysquat.

He's a rebel without a clue.

By the way, the only folks he hangs around are those whom he upstages in talent or family members who make excuses for his obstinacy and who have to love him because of the whole family-genetic-"he's blood"-thing.

> **Pussies don't listen to wise counsel. Listen to and heed wisdom.**

Don't be like that guy.

Check it out: Evolving bad-asses are secure in their bad-assedness.

They know they don't know it all.

They realize they're a piece of the puzzle and not the puzzle.

This makes them a sponge for info, wisdom, knowledge and discipline even when it makes them feel stupid, wrong and lazy in certain areas.

Indeed, those who're moving out of Pussville and into Mantown don't mind these temporary personal pains and inconveniences delivered by bad-asses who have already mastered big chunks of their life.

> **Be a sponge for wisdom. Soak it all up!.**

So... what's the reason why they can roll with the punches delivered by the great ones?

Well... it's this, Crispin.

They're teachable, unlike all the petulant metros. And they're teachable even when the lessons are raw and entail stiff rebuke.

Yep, they don't run and hide like a pussy.

They don't try to vilify the one delivering the personal rebuke bombs.

They take the punch on the chin if it's true and they learn and grow, unlike the whiny sister pussies who instead isolate, blame-shift and remain stunted in their growth, and end up being the High Priest of the one-man cult called The Church of I'm an Un-teachable Pussy.

Why do you live on Shame Street in the heart of Pussville?

It's because you're unwilling to stomp maximum ass in your endeavors.

~Doug Giles

Chapter 18

Go Balls Out

Go Balls Out.

I'm a big advocate of living balls-out. Matter of fact, I'm going balls-out right now as I write this book.

No, I'm not talking about wearing shorts that are so short and open at the crotch that my newly grey-haired boys are clearly visible to the shock and awe of the passersby in the coffee shop I'm writing in.

Indeed, when I say I'm living "balls-out" I mean it in the way the phrase was used back in the day. For the uninformed, the phrase "balls-out" refers to the governor on an old steam engine. Two heavy balls are attached to the engine so that as engine speed increases, the centrifugal force of the flywheel causes the balls to rise. As the balls top out, they govern (limit) the engine, thereby controlling maximum engine speed. "Balls-out", then, refers to running the engine at maximum speed.

That's what I'm talking about. Namely, you... running... at... maximum speed. Giving whatever your hand finds to do with all of your heart. I'm talkin' about getting intense with your pursuits.

Pussies don't know squat about this kind of moxie and it's a mega-reason why they dwell on Shame Street in the heart of Pussville; because they're unwilling to stomp maximum ass in their endeavors.

A man once described Generation Pussy as apathetic and cynical: always willing to believe the worst as long as it takes as little effort as possible.

From an energy and outlook standpoint, I concur with his assessment.

All Generation Pussy does is blather about how bad they have it as they play Xbox marathons from the fat lap of American luxury. And I mean fat.

Yeah… you boys have it so bad. I now get why your weltanschauung is more jaded than Kimora's jewelry box.

Poor, poor, poor me.

Poor, poor, pitiful me.

This "eff it all" attitude seems to have had an adverse effect upon their energy levels because zealous this generation is not.

> Going "balls out" is not a crotch thing. Get educated!

Matter of fact, if you're looking for spunk from these punks then you're going to be woefully disappointed because it… ain't… there.

I've seen dying manatees floundering around in the nasty, shallow and steamy, black swamp water of the Oleta River State Park show more verve than these slow motion me-monkeys.

Case in point, just now I rocked up to this coffee shop to get a cup of Java and work on this book where I'm trying to help present pussies move from a loathsome state of male ineptitude to something that somewhat resembles an accomplished man in the classic sense of the word.

Check it out: there were only two customers at the counter ordering coffee, me and this other chick. Only two. Like in one… two.

Guess how long it took me and the other girl to get a cup of coffee? If you guessed ten minutes, then you guessed right.

It took me ten minutes to get a cup of coffee. I ain't got time to wait ten minutes. I'm busy, brother.

The infuriating thing was this dude didn't have to brew a new pot. He didn't have to wash two dirty mugs. He didn't have go to Colombia to find Juan Valdez and his frickin' donkey wandering the mountains outside of Bogota and bum some beans off him to cook us a sweet pot of Joe. And we didn't order some kind of funky caffeinated drink that took a biblical time, times and half a time for four baristas to make. All this male had to do was grab two cups, fill them up, and then hand the mugs to us.

> Manhood is measured in minutes - not inches.

That's it.

How long can this possibly take?

The guy working the counter looked to be twenty-five years old but he moved slower than a Bob Dole bowel movement.

Seriously... only two customers and he's just lurching around behind the counter.

Oh, and I almost forgot, he was texting before, during and after serving us.

Here's an FYI to dipsticks working in the service industry: the customer is profit and you're overhead. Guess who's more important?

> People who work hard make their own luck.

As you can tell I hate, and I mean hate, half-heartedness, apathy and passivity.

Look, whatever your excuse is for being a dejected, weepy sleestack, you need to scrub it if you want to move from Pussville to Mantown, young Crispin.

I don't care how sucky your job is or how bleak your future looks. What I've found in fifty-plus years of kickin' dirt on this blue marble is the harder I work the "luckier" I get.

You gotta go full bore with everything you do.

Whole heartedness... hard and smart work.... with the task at hand… is the way out of Pussville and into the city limits of Mantown.

Take my advice, young squab, and crucify any and all proclivities to laziness and half-assedness and I guarantee your life will tick up every year.

Go balls-out or get used to living in the sad, dank, unaccomplished, mediocre world of Pussville.

Oh, and just one other thing, please… don't ever say a word about why you don't have this or that as long as you reject the balls-out attitude.

Also, don't rag on people who are prosperous and enjoying life. They probably made a conscious decision to both reject passivity and live courageously; and thus they should be rewarded, you envious little joke of a man.

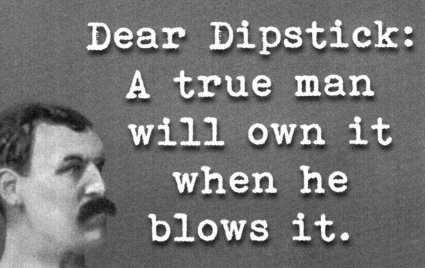

Dear Dipstick:
A true man
will own it
when he
blows it.

A pussy blames
others for his
screw ups.

~Doug Giles

Chapter 19

Quit Passing

The Buck

Quit Passing the Buck

Nobody's responsible for anything anymore.

Just ask them.

They'll tell you real quick that it's not their fault and it's not their job... man.

From 1600 Pennsylvania Avenue to West Florissant Avenue, the buck gets passed on more than Larry the Cable Guy does when he auditions for a Victoria's Secret open call.

Our current milieu is smegma rich with blame-shifting and responsibility eschewing.

Ain't nobody got time for responsibility.

One sure-fire way, Crispin, to separate from the pusillanimous pack and get well on your way out of Pussville and down to the mean streets of Mantown is to take the masculine path of... drum roll please... responsibility.

For the pussies who aren't familiar with the term or the thought of being responsible, the word "responsible" is an adjective which means: having the job or duty of dealing with or taking care of something or someone.

It means to be trusted to do what is right or to do the things that are expected or required, usually involving important duties, decisions, etc., that are entrusted to you.

And guess what, ladies and genitals … Pussies hate that stuff. And I mean hate.

Selling responsibility to today's dillweeds is much akin to selling Rosie O'Donnell on skinny vodka and low fat Bean Dip.

It.

Ain't.

Gonna.

Happen.

So… why do the vast multitudes of young rabble scram from accountability?

I think it's due largely in part because their Boomer and GenX predecessors sacrificed true greatness on the altar of rank narcissism and its spawn, self-preservation; of which their me-monkey children were all but too happy to embrace with greater zeal.

For example, check out Generation Pussy's "authority" figures.

During Obama's two torrid terms, he wasn't responsible for anything negative. Like in nada.

Indeed, BHO's admin has been indelibly marked by accelerated financial debt, foreign policy bungles, scandals aplenty, a coddling of terrorists, rank racial tensions, an antipathy for law enforcement and our military and an overall disintegration of our nation's exceptionalism.

> People will trust you if you are responsible.

But… it's not Barack's fault if you were to ask him. Oh, hell no. It's Bush's fault.

Yep, even though it's been he and his feckless policies in place for the last eight long-ass years, he's not to blame for it, but George W is.

And that, my friends, is what is called "passing the buck."

Speaking of douches, the House and Senate don't give a rat's ass if they don't do what they were elected and/or needed to do for the good of our country. Screw that noise. They're too busy milking special interest groups and their interns' sex organs to actually be bothered with performing the jobs we were dumb enough to elect them to do.

While I'm on the topic of irresponsibility, did you know the lardy hagfish, also known as Hillary Rodham Clinton, is "not responsible" for letting our ambassador Chris Stevens and our best of the best be butchered in Benghazi?

If you think I'm full of bollocks, just ask The Hildebeest. She'll tell you it ain't her fault and she'll blame it on an unwatched YouTube video... or poor communication... or low blood sugar... or global warming... or the Vast Right Wing Conspiracy. That's it! The Conservatives made her not send military support for Stevens and his crew when they begged #CrookedHillary to launch sorties on their behalf. There... see how easy that was?

Now, when discussing blame-shifting, one cannot talk about passing the buck and not bring up the brethren.

Have you ever noticed that when pastors and priests get caught squat-humping an altar boy that it's never their fault?

What's their excuse?

For those that are a part of the flock that's an easy question, eh?

C'mon... you know what ministers say when they're busted red-handed don't you?

> BHO passes the buck more often than a sated grizzly in Alaska.

Think hard.

Who do they blame?

Here's a hint: A little naughty dude... with a red suit... and a pitchfork... cloven hoofs... and a goatee? Ring any bells? No, not Kanye West. Think deeper. Do you give up? They blame the devil for all their bad choices.

"The devil made them do it."

The devil made you do it?

The hell, you say.

How convenient.

From politicians to pastors, no one's to blame for their god-awful decisions or dilatory behavior and, ergo, responsibility gets tossed around like a drunken midget in a Metallica mosh pit with these Millennials.

Oh, I almost forgot. Did you know that postmodern parents aren't responsible for horrendously failing on their job of raising the next generation? They'll blame our crap-laden culture, or porn, or our paranormal school system, or a lawless society, or a too restrictive and repressive puritanical landscape. Y'know... something other than the fact that they shoved off their kids to a nanny because mommy was obsessing on Facebook.

> Take responsibility for your mistakes and people will respect you.

Speaking of our "schools", my wife taught in public schools for seventeen years and she said that parents of the "bad kids" were way more jacked up than their poor children.

Yes, most of today's parents suck at parenting; and yes I'm talking about you.

Indeed, if your kid is mucked up, then look further than your mirror and blame yourself for obsessing on social media while little Sally and Mikey were ignored.

One more little ditty for those who want to procreate or who have procreated: if you bring a child into this world it is your job to make certain said kid doesn't morph into the saggy-panted dipstick that I nearly ran over, who was texting while he was walking across the I-95 while smoking the devil's lettuce.

Granted, young Crispin, even though running from responsibility might momentarily extract you from the angst of feeling like an F-up, which is a necessary and innate punitive emotion for when one has dropped the proverbial ball, it will also, in the long run, keep you from true leadership and greatness which requires a hearty embracing of accountability.

Memorize this maxim, dear pussy: Responsibility is the gateway to greatness in all spheres of life.

If you're given a job, duty or task ... then do it.

Yes, it will cost you blood, sweat and tears.

Yes, you will fail sometimes, oft times, in accomplishing the task at hand, but that's the path to Mantown.

In addition, please note: A true man will own it when he blows it. A man won't blame others for his screw ups.

> Own your mistakes and make them work for you.

Do you know who's responsible for all of my failings in life? My dad because he didn't buy me baseball cards like my buddy Robert's dad used to.

Sorry, I kind of lost it there for a second and tapped into the spirit de puss.

No, all the horrible hobbles throughout my life were caused by moi. Sure, I'd love to blame others and metaphysical, malevolent forces, but at the end of the day, no one but my stupid self made me do stupid things. Mea culpa. Sure, such a confession makes me feel bad, but the admission that it was me helps me, knowing that I can't change much but I can change me.

Lastly, as you embrace responsibility and you succeed in life, there's nothing wrong with feeling proud of your accomplishment because you fought the good fight of being a man; so, therefore, always walk into a room with your head held high.

Addendum

The 10 Commandments for Pussies Who Want to Date Your Daughter

The 10 Commandments for Pussies Who Want to Date Your Daughter

God, in His providence, has seen fit to bestow upon my wife and me two beautiful girls that we must steward into greatness. It has been a blast watching my daughters develop into righteous and rowdy, gorgeous girls. The thing that sucks with their metamorphosis into womanhood is the guys who've begun to buzz around our happy nest interested in my ladies.

As much as I don't like the idea of their dating, I have got to suck it up and accept it (bartender, I'll have a shot of whiskey). All you dads who are worth your salt and give a crap about your kid...you know how hard it is to let your girls go. (I'll take another shot, please.)

Even though I'm slowly coming to grips with my kids growing up, I'm not throwing out my brain and becoming a hip and groovy dad who curls up in the corner in the fetal position without an opinion regarding their dating life.

Not only do I have an opinion regarding wannabe suitors, I have ten commandments for potential boyfriends. Yes, seeing that I'm still the Alpha dog of the Giles castle, that I still pay the bills, buy the SUVs, pay for college and secure their condos, then by God, I'm still makin' the rules. I am Doug Almighty, got that Rico Suave? What I'm about to reveal unto you is an attitude-laden afflatus, so...be afraid. Herewith are my 10 commandments for my daughter's potential boyfriends. Read them and weep:

1. Thou shall understand that your presence doesn't make me happy. Young squire, don't expect me to be giggly when I meet you. As a matter of fact, you're ruining my life right now. Therefore, don't try to be cute with me. That stuff may work on my daughter or my wife, but it does not work with me.

   Actually, you should expect nothing from me in the way of the warm and fuzzies. You've got to earn that. I don't care who you are or who your momma is. Your presence represents a transition that I'm not really ready for, so just stay the heck back and be real cool. And know this: I've got a PI doing a background check on you right now.

2. Thou had better have a life. My wife and I have worked our tails off providing a good life for our girls; therefore, you better have one, Spanky. Let me spell it out for you just in case you don't get it. You must have something positive going on in that thing you call a life.

   Additionally, you must be pursuing said noble goal at Mach 2 with your hair on fire. If you're a slacking, blame-shifting, visionless slug with genital warts who's waiting for someone to carry you into greatness and who lives by the dictates of his ding dong, then you need to find a girl who doesn't have a father like me.

3. Thou shall not touch my daughter, or I'll tear your hands off and you'll have to "whip the bishop" with a stub. Not only am I not cool with your being around me, I'm sure as heck not down with you touching my daughter. Therefore, when you're in my space (and in my absence) you'd better treat my daughters with the utmost respect.

   Do not under any circumstance hang all over my daughter, fondle my daughter or soul kiss my kid until you have a wedding ring on her finger, a joint checking account and MMA at

Wachovia—or I will shove your Justin Timberlake backside off my 3rd floor balcony first chance I get, capisce?

4. Thou shall look me in the eye, shake my hand like a man and turn off your damn cell phone. I don't care how Snoop Dog acts and what you've seen on MTV or in the movies. If you come into my house mumbling, with your shades on and texting the entire time you're around me, you're probably going to be spending the next couple of days in ICU.

    I want eye contact. I want you to see my soul, son. I want to look you in the eye when I communicate things regarding my girls and their lives. So, take the shades off, Hollywood. In addition, if and when I extend my hand, grab it like you mean it. Where I come from, a limp hand shake = limp life, Twinkle Toes. Also, when you're at my casa, your phone goes on vibrate. I'm sure you'll like that.

5. Thou shall understand that you are a boy talking to a man. Here's some 411 to meditate upon before you address me. I am at least twice your age. I used to be a drug user/dealer until God zapped me. I've been in many fights. I've shot at felons. I faced down too many to count charging wild boar. I've spent years in Tae Kwon Do. I've traveled the planet. You, on the other hand, use Proactiv and drive a Ford Focus; therefore, you will call me "Mr. Giles" and my wife "Mrs. Giles" until we tell you any different.

    Also, don't gush around me nor attempt to read me an entry from your journal. I'm not Oprah or one of your metrosexual buddies that you can share all of your inner fears and deepest needs with. I am a Neanderthal.

6. Thou shall know that our family is old school. Do not even think about approaching me with liberal, hippy, agnostic, atheistic, anti-American or tree-humping bull crap. I was raised by country-loving, God-fearing, hard-working, meat-eating, good ole' Texan parents, and I have zero toler-

ance for what your long-toothed, rather mannish lesbian so-
ciology teacher at Columbia U programmed you with—you
dig?

7. Thou shall know that I like cool and expensive gifts, and
you shall provide unto me this bounty, if you're smart.
One great way to earn my favor is to buy it. Yes, you'd
be shrewd to approach me like the three wise men did
baby Jesus, namely with gold, frankincense and myrrh.

For example, I like high-quality cigars (nothing below a
90), Johnnie Walker Blue Label, Chimay Grand Reserve,
books on hunting Africa and old British double rifles. I
also like original art work, R&B and classic rock compila-
tions, collecting skulls, hunting and big game fishing trips,
antique Christian and Classic books, custom choppers
and early twentieth century African safari memorabilia.

Who knows...I might, might, ask you to join me for a nice
cigar session with me and the boys if thou comest bearing
such offerings.

8. Thou shall understand that if you're dumb enough to tell me
a dirty joke, I'm comfortable enough with kicking your butt.
I'm not one of your thug buddies you can go down the gutter
with. I want maturity when you are around my family.

9. Thou shall keep your word. If you say you're going to do
something, then I expect you to do it. You see, I'm looking
for stability/reliability for my ladies, and keeping your word
in the smallest matters tells me that you're ahead of the pack
and at least a consideration, in my mind, for our support.

10. Thou shall do these three things:
1) Look good. Do not come into my house with earrings, a
grill, or oversized pants with your butt cleavage hanging
out.
2) Read. If I have to talk to you, you had better know as

much about as many things as possible.

3) Serve. I'm looking for a sacrificial dude who doesn't mind getting his hands dirty in helping around the house, in our community, in our nation and with our wonderful world. If you, young man, obey all the words written here, then and only then will you have a chance with my babies. Now, go get me a beer!

About the Author

Doug Giles is the man behind ClashDaily.com. In addition to driving ClashDaily.com, Giles is the author of eight books including his best-seller, *Raising Righteous and Rowdy Girls.*

Doug's articles have also appeared on several other print and online news sources, including *Townhall.com, The Washington Times, The Daily Caller, Fox Nation, USA Today, The Wall Street Journal, The Washington Examiner, American Hunter* magazine and *ABC News.*

Giles and his wife Margaret have two daughters: Hannah, who devastated ACORN with her 2009 nation-shaking undercover videos, and Regis who is a huntress, and owner of GirlsJustWanna-HaveGuns.com

DG's interests include guns, big game hunting, big game fishing, fine art, cigars, helping wounded warriors, and being a big pain in the butt to people who dislike God and the USA.

Accolades for Giles and ClashDaily.com include ...

– Giles was recognized as one of "The 50 Best Conservative Columnists of 2015"

– Giles was recognized as one of "The 50 Best Conservative Columnists of 2014"

– Giles was recognized as one of "The 50 Best Conservative Columnists of 2013"

– ClashDaily.com was recognized as one of "The 100 Most Popular Conservative Websites For 2013"

– Doug was noted as "Hot Conservative New Media Superman" By Politichicks

Speaking Engagements.

Doug Giles speaks to college, business, community, church, advocacy and men's groups throughout the United States and internationally. His expertise includes issues of Christianity and culture, masculinity vs. metrosexuality, big game hunting and fishing, raising righteous kids in a rank culture, the Second Amendment, personal empowerment, politics, and social change. Giles charges $5,000 per speaking engagement, plus food, hotel and travel expenses. For availability, please contact us at clash@clashdaily.com. Please use 'SPEAKING ENGAGEMENT' for your subject line when sending your request.

Other books by Doug Giles

Raising Righteous and Rowdy Girls

Raising Boys Feminists Will Hate

Ruling in Babylon: Seven Habits of Highly Effective Twenty-somethings

Political Twerps, Cultural Jerks, Church Quirks

The Bulldog Attitude: Get It or Get Left Behind

10 Habits of Decidedly Defective People: The Successful Loser's Guide to Life

A Time to Clash: Papers from a Provocative Pastor

If You're Going Through Hell Keep on Going

Coming the fall of 2017

Hunting and The Bible:
Is God Against Putting
The Bam To Bambi?

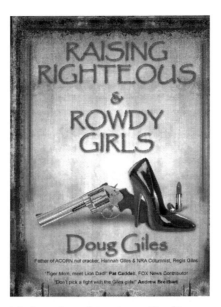

It has been said that daughters are God's revenge on fathers for the kind of men they were when they were young. Some would say that both Doug Giles and I, given our infamous pasts, are charter members of that club. However, Doug and I know that his two wonderful daughters and my equally wonderful daughter and two granddaughters are truly God's fantastic gift. With the wisdom of hindsight and experience Doug has written the ultimate manual for dads on raising righteous and rowdy daughters who will go out into the world well prepared- morally, physically, intellectually and with joyful hearts- to be indomitable and mighty lionesses in our cultural jungle. Through every raucous and no-holds-barred page, Doug, the incomparable Dad Drill Sergeant, puts mere men through the paces to join the ranks of the few, the proud, and the successful fathers of super daughters. The proof of Doug Giles' gold-plated credentials are Hannah and Regis Giles- two of the most fantastic, great hearted and accomplished young ladies I have ever known. This is THE BOOK that I will be giving the father of my two precious five and three year old granddaughters. Tiger Mom meet Lion Dad!

— Pat Caddell

Fox News Contributor —

40154815R00114

Made in the USA
San Bernardino, CA
12 October 2016